Revised Edition

T5-BQB-504

Who Are the Urban Poor?

by ANTHONY DOWNS

Supplementary Paper Number 26

COMMITTEE FOR ECONOMIC DEVELOPMENT

iv

Soc
HC
110
P6
D63
1970

LIBRARY
FLORIDA STATE UNIVERSITY
TALLAHASSEE, FLORIDA

COPYRIGHT © 1970 *by the* Committee for Economic Development.

All rights reserved. No part of this book may be
reproduced or utilized in any form or by any means,
electronic or mechanical, including photocopying, re-
cording, or by any information storage or retrieval
system, without permission in writing from the Committee for Economic Development, 477 Madison
Avenue, New York, New York 10022.

Printed in the U.S.A.
First printing, October, 1968.
Second printing, February, 1969.
Revised edition, September, 1970.

COMMITTEE FOR ECONOMIC DEVELOPMENT
477 Madison Avenue, New York, N. Y. 10022
Library of Congress Catalog Card Number 77-133484

Who Are the Urban Poor?

WHO CARES?

I do!

6

I don't

JESUS CARES!!

"BLESSED ARE THE POOR IN SPIRIT, FOR THEY WILL INHERIT THE KINGDOM OF GOD"

The Author

ANTHONY DOWNS received a bachelor of arts degree, summa cum laude, in political theory and international relations from Carleton College in 1952 and a doctor of philosophy degree in economics from Stanford University in 1956. He joined the Real Estate Research Corporation of Chicago on a part-time basis at the age of seventeen and became a full-time associate in 1959. He is now senior vice president and treasurer. Downs is a consultant on urban affairs and government organization to the RAND Corporation. He has been a consultant to the National Advisory Commission on Civil Disorders and to numerous public and private organizations. He has served on the faculty of the University of Chicago in the economics and political science departments; he has also lectured at Harvard University, the University of California at Berkeley, and other leading universities. Downs is the author of two books—*An Economic Theory of Democracy* and *Inside Bureaucracy*—and of many articles and reviews. He is currently a member of the President's National Commission on Urban Problems.

A CED SUPPLEMENTARY PAPER

This Supplementary Paper is issued by the Research and Policy Committee of the Committee for Economic Development in conformity with the CED Bylaws (Art. V, Sec. 6), which authorize the publication of a manuscript as a Supplementary Paper if:

a) It is recommended for publication by the Project Director of a subcommittee because in his opinion, it "constitutes an important contribution to the understanding of a problem on which research has been initiated by the Research and Policy Committee" and,

b) It is approved for publication by a majority of an Editorial Board on the ground that it presents "an analysis which is a significant contribution to the understanding of the problem in question."

This Supplementary Paper relates to the Statement on National Policy, *Raising Low Incomes Through Improved Education,* issued by the CED Research and Policy Committee in September 1965.

The members of the Editorial Board authorizing publication of this Supplementary Paper are:

CHARLES KELLER, JR. **JOSEPH L. BLOCK**	*Members of the Research and Policy Committee* *of the Committee for Economic Development*
T. W. SCHULTZ **PAUL YLVISAKER**	*Member, CED Research Advisory Board* *Associate Member, CED Research Advisory Board*
ALFRED C. NEAL	*President of the Committee* *for Economic Development*
LYLE C. FITCH	*Project Director of the CED Subcommittee* *on Problems of Urban Poverty*

This paper has also been read by the Research Advisory Board, the members of which under the CED Bylaws may submit memoranda of comment, reservation, or dissent.

While publication of this Supplementary Paper is authorized by CED's Bylaws, except as noted above its contents have not been approved, disapproved, or acted upon by the Committee for Economic Development, the Board of Trustees, the Research and Policy Committee, the Research Advisory Board, the Research Staff, or any member of any board or committee, or any officer of the Committee for Economic Development.

CED RESEARCH ADVISORY BOARD
(as of October 1968)

Chairman

EDWARD S. MASON
Lamont University Professor
Harvard University

J. DOUGLAS BROWN
Provost and Dean of the Faculty
    Emeritus
Princeton University

OTTO ECKSTEIN
Department of Economics
Harvard University

KERMIT GORDON
President
The Brookings Institution

ARNOLD HARBERGER
Department of Economics
University of Chicago

CHARLES P. KINDLEBERGER
Department of Economics and
    Social Science
Massachusetts Institute of Technology

DANIEL P. MOYNIHAN
Director, Joint Center for Urban Studies
    of the Massachusetts Institute of
    Technology and Harvard University

WALLACE S. SAYRE
Chairman
Department of Political Science
Columbia University

T. W. SCHULTZ
Department of Economics
University of Chicago

DONALD C. STONE
Dean, Graduate School of Public
    and International Affairs
University of Pittsburgh

MITCHELL SVIRIDOFF
Vice President
Division of National Affairs
The Ford Foundation

RAYMOND VERNON
Professor of International Trade and
    Investment, Graduate School of
    Business Administration
Harvard University

Associate Members

WALTER W. HELLER
Department of Economics
University of Minnesota

FRITZ MACHLUP
Director
International Finance Section
Princeton University

GEORGE P. SHULTZ
Dean, Graduate School of Business
University of Chicago

PAUL YLVISAKER
Commissioner
New Jersey State Department of
    Community Affairs

Foreword

The Committee for Economic Development has been at work on problems of the nation's metropolitan areas for nearly a decade, and during that period it has published a number of significant studies that remain classics in their fields. These include Supplementary Papers such as Raymond Vernon's *The Changing Economic Function of the Central City* and Robert C. Wood's *Metropolis Against Itself;* and Statements on National Policy such as *Guiding Metropolitan Growth* and *Raising Low Incomes Through Improved Education.*

The present supplementary paper stems from the renewed interest of CED in problems of poverty, particularly as they relate to urban areas. This interest has resulted in the recent policy statements on *Improving the Public Welfare System* and *Training and Jobs for the Urban Poor.* At the commencement of these studies, CED's Subcommittee on Problems of Urban Poverty expressed a desire to know more about the dimensions of poverty—who the poverty-stricken are, where they are located, how many there are, and why they are poor. The subcommittee therefore commissioned Anthony Downs to prepare this report on the varied aspects of urban poverty. Downs is an urban scholar of wide reputation and a consultant to many government agencies and commissions.

Poverty is an elusive concept, difficult to define. The task of developing appropriate new policies to combat poverty is therefore quite formidable. Downs' findings have eased that task considerably, for he has put together in a systematic way a vast amount of fresh data on this difficult subject. His paper has proved to be of great value in CED's ongoing work in this field, particularly in the preparation of the recent statement on the welfare system. The data contained in the paper, it was felt, would be useful not only to the CED subcommittees working in this area but also to businessmen and scholars, government officials and community leaders everywhere—in short, to all who are dealing with problems of urban poverty. The paper was therefore given wider publication, and the general response has been such that the data has now been updated in this revised edition in accordance with the latest census figures.

I would like to express my gratitude to Downs for preparing this study; to Lyle C. Fitch, the subcommittee's Project Director, for providing the introduction; to Sol Hurwitz, CED Director of Information, for helping to prepare this volume for publication; and to Seong Park, of the CED Research Staff, for his assistance in revising the data for this edition.

Charles Keller, Jr., *Chairman*
Subcommittee on Problems of Urban Poverty

Introduction

This paper brings together a wealth of data and information, not hitherto assembled, which illuminates today's most difficult and perplexing domestic problem. Anthony Downs' report clarifies the concept of poverty among individuals and families, presents estimates of the numbers in each group, and suggests reasons why they are poor. The paper sets right many prevalent misconceptions about poverty, including the misconception that poverty stems primarily from laziness and lack of ambition and initiative. Of the 10 per cent of the total metropolitan-area population who were poor in 1968, more than half were the very old, the very young, and the sick and disabled. Nearly half were in households that cannot be expected to become economically self-sustaining. Nearly one-third were in households with regularly employed heads under sixty-five, whose poverty stems primarily from low earnings.

These are striking figures. Equally striking is the concept of poverty itself. The concept used in this paper, largely because it is the only one for which adequate data are available, rests on a food-based budget of the Social Security Administration—the line between poverty and nonpoverty is set at three times the cost of minimal food requirements. As Downs emphasizes, this is a conservative definition of poverty. The number of people in poverty, so defined, is relatively small and has been diminishing over recent years. Even so, the number of poverty-stricken in 1968 was approximately 25 million in the nation, almost 13 million of which were in metropolitan areas.

The classification of poor persons goes far to explain the causes of poverty:

Elderly (sixty-five or over)

Children (under eighteen)

Adults in female-headed households (eighteen to sixty-four)

Adults in households headed by disabled males (eighteen to sixty-four)

Adults in households headed by unemployed males (eighteen to sixty-four)

Adults in households headed by employed males (eighteen to sixty-four)

While this is not a paper on policy, it does lay bare a number of basic policy issues. The issue which has been of most concern to businessmen recently has been training and jobs. A second major set of issues arises out of the present unsatisfactory state of welfare and other forms of income maintenance and out of the rising demand for substantial improvement, as, for example, through some device such as a negative income tax. The third set of issues has to do with removing or reducing the many institutional factors that now militate against self-sufficiency and therefore tend to perpetuate poverty. A fourth set has to do with concentration of the poor, particularly of minority racial and ethnic groups, in central-city ghettos while major growth is occurring outside central cities. Finally, a fifth set of issues concerns health, as it bears on productivity of workers and pupils and on the needs of the aged and others not in the working force.

Lyle C. Fitch, *Project Director*
President, Institute of Public Administration

Contents

Foreword   vii

Introduction   ix

1. Summary of Factual Findings   1

2. What is Poverty?   6

   The Poverty "Threshold"　6

   Replacing the Current Definition　9

3. The Extent of Urban Poverty   13

4. Specific Types of Urban Poverty   18

   The Elderly Poor　19

   Poor Children Under Eighteen　24

   Poor Households Headed by Females　31

   Poor Households Headed by
      Disabled Males Under Sixty-five　36

   Poor Households Headed by Non-disabled
      but Unemployed Males Under Sixty-five　37

   Poor Households Headed by
      Employed Males Under Sixty-five　38

5. How Social Institutions Reinforce Poverty   44

6. Future Population Changes and the Urban Poor   50

   Over-all Population Trends　51

   Specific Population Trends　53

7. Policy Issues   58

   Notes   61

1. Summary of Factual Findings

The following significant findings and conclusions can be drawn from the extensive data and analysis presented in the body of this paper.

1. *Poverty in the United States is officially measured by a fixed standard of real income based upon the cost of a minimal human diet. But the concept of poverty is actually quite complex and controversial; so all statistics concerning it must be used and interpreted with caution.*

—Any household is officially defined as "poor" by the Social Security Administration if its annual money income is less than three times the cost (in current prices) of a minimal diet for the persons in that household. In 1968 the "poverty level" income for a four-person (nonfarm) household was $3,553.

—In comparison with the incomes of much of the world's population, many Americans considered poor by this definition are actually quite well-off. On the other hand, official "poverty level" incomes are very low in comparison with either the nation's median family income (of $8,362 in 1968) or the income considered necessary for a "moderate" standard of living by the Bureau of Labor Statistics (over $9,600 in 1968 dollars for a four-person household).

Author's Acknowledgment: Particular credit goes to Seong Park, of the CED Research Staff, who was responsible for bringing the statistics up to date for the present edition of this paper and for revising the text in accordance with the new data. Several members of my staff at the Systemetrics Division of Real Estate Research Corporation also made key contributions to this paper. Richard Engler gathered and initially analyzed the data. Joanne Smith checked the calculations for accuracy, and Kay Mulligan typed the manuscript.

—Since the official definition of poverty is based upon an absolutely fixed level of income, continued national prosperity that raises all incomes in society inevitably causes the number of poor people to decline steadily. But if poverty is considered a *relative* matter, its disadvantages will continue to affect all people in the lowest income groups, unless there is a significant change in the *distribution* of income (which has not occurred in recent years).

All statistics concerning poverty in this paper are based upon the official Social Security Administration definition.

2. *In 1968 about 10.0 per cent of the total metropolitan-area population of the United States—or 12.9 million persons—lived in poverty.*

—This was somewhat lower than the percentage of all U.S. citizens in poverty (12.8 per cent), and much lower than comparable figures for any nonmetropolitan areas.

—Nevertheless, slightly over half of all poor persons in the United States lived in metropolitan areas in 1968.

3. *Within metropolitan areas, the proportion of poor people in 1968 was almost twice as high in central cities (13.4 per cent) as in suburbs (7.3 per cent).* Although more people lived in suburbs, the number of poor persons in central cities (7.8 million) was significantly larger than in suburbs (5.1 million).

4. *About two-thirds of all the poor persons in metropolitan areas in 1968 were white, and one-third nonwhite. However, the proportion of all metropolitan-area whites who were poor (7.6 per cent) was less than one-third the proportion of such nonwhites who were poor (25.7 per cent).*

—About 76 per cent of the poor nonwhites and 52 per cent of the poor whites in metropolitan areas lived in central cities.

—Within central cities, 57 per cent of all poor persons were white, and 43 per cent nonwhite. But 80 per cent of all poor suburbanites were white.

5. *From 1959 to 1968, the total number of poor persons in the United States declined by 14.1 million (or by 36 per cent)*

from 39.5 million to 25.4 million. In the same period, the number of poor living in metropolitan areas decreased by 4.1 million (or by 24 per cent) from 17.0 million to 12.9 million. Because of the migration of rural poor to the nation's urban centers and a faster population increase there, the percentage decline of poor persons was less in metropolitan areas than in nonmetropolitan areas. Among the metropolitan poor, whites decreased more rapidly than nonwhites. Furthermore, most of this decrease in the metropolitan poor took place among households headed by men. Poor persons living in male-headed households decreased nearly half between 1959 and 1968. But those in households headed by women actually increased (by 22 per cent) in this period. These trends were also evident for the nation as a whole.

6. *About 47 per cent of all poor in metropolitan areas are in households that cannot be expected to become economically self-sustaining at any time in the future.*[1]
    These households include:

Type of Household Head	Per Cent of All Poor Persons in Metropolitan Areas
Elderly	18.3%
Disabled males under sixty-five	4.5
Females under sixty-five with children	23.7
TOTAL	46.5

7. *Nearly one-fourth of all poor persons in metropolitan areas (24.5 per cent) are in households headed by regularly employed men under sixty-five whose poverty results from low earnings rather than unemployment, disability, or old age.*

8. *About one-eighth of all metropolitan-area poor are in households headed by non-disabled men under sixty-five who are either unemployed or underemployed.*

9. *About 5.4 million poor people in metropolitan areas— or 42.2 per cent of all such people in 1968—were children under*

eighteen. The poverty in which they lived is likely to afflict them in such a way as to reduce their future income-earning capabilities.

—Almost two-thirds of these poor children lived in central cities, and over half the poor children in those cities were nonwhite.

—From 43 to 56 per cent of all poor children in metropolitan areas lived in households unlikely to become economically self-sustaining.

—Poor children are heavily concentrated in large families. In the United States as a whole, 44 per cent of all poor children in 1968 were in families with five or more children.

10. *Although poverty is technically defined as having a very low annual income, for many people it is also a chronic state of failure, disability, dependency, defeat, and inability to share in most of American society's major material and spiritual benefits. Their continuance in this deprived state is reinforced by many institutional arrangements in our society, including those supposedly designed to aid them.*

11. *Future population changes in metropolitan areas are likely to cause certain groups with a high incidence of poverty, particularly within central cities, to expand greatly. Whether this will result in any increase in the number of poor persons depends upon future public policies and prosperity levels.*

—The greatest *absolute* growth from 1960 to 1985 will occur in the following "poverty-prone" population groups: suburban, white elderly; central-city, nonwhite children under eighteen; central-city, nonwhite households with female heads under sixty-five; and white and nonwhite households headed by unemployed males under sixty-five in both central cities and suburbs.

—Large absolute growth will also occur among suburban white children under eighteen—probably adding as many as one million of these children to urban poverty by 1985.

—The nonwhite population of all U.S. central cities is expected to rise by 9.8 million—or 94.5 per cent—from 1960 to 1985. Since this population contains many highly "poverty-prone" groups, such rapid growth could cause sharp increases in nonwhite poverty within central cities—especially in the largest cities where, in many cases, nonwhites will form a majority of the population by 1985. But major rises in nonwhite poverty will probably not occur unless there are significant and substantial lapses from high-level prosperity—thus causing higher unemployment and lower incomes for many partly-employed workers—or unless there is an acceleration of the recent trend toward a rise in the number of families headed by women with young children.

2. What is Poverty?

Most people think of poverty as simply having very little money. In fact, this criterion is the basis for official statistical studies of how many people are poor, mainly because of the difficulty of obtaining accurate information relevant to any other definition.

Yet considering poverty as just lack of money is misleading, especially when one is trying to discover how to reduce it. Most people with very little money have low capabilities for earning income. Thus, low income-earning capability rather than lack of money should be the key focal point for remedial policies.

The causes of low income-earning capability leading to poverty vary so widely that the poor must be divided into several separate groups for the purpose of analysis:

1. The elderly—aged persons in family units and unrelated individuals sixty-five and over.
2. Children under eighteen.
3. Households headed by females under sixty-five.
4. Households headed by disabled males under sixty-five.
5. Households headed by nondisabled men under sixty-five who are either unemployed or underemployed.
6. Households headed by nondisabled men under sixty-five who are regularly employed but earn low incomes.[2]

The Poverty "Threshold"

Data used in this paper concerning the number of poor persons in each of these categories are based upon definitions of poverty worked out by the Social Security Administration. These definitions are essentially food-oriented. That is, a certain minimum human diet was assigned current costs every year. It was then somewhat arbitrarily assumed that any household that had to spend more than one-third of its income to procure this minimum diet was poor. So a poverty "threshold" was calculated for a household according to its size by tripling the cost of providing the minimum diet for the number of persons. (A slightly different procedure was used for farm families, but we can disregard this difference.) Any household of a given size with an annual income less than this threshold is considered poor.[3]

Most of the poverty data in this paper are for 1968. The poverty income thresholds for that year are shown in Table 1.[4] Whether these incomes should be considered high or low depends upon the standard of comparison used. In relation to what most of the world's population receives, these incomes are quite high. International income comparisons can be misleading, especially when data from different time periods are

Table 1. **Nonfarm Poverty Threshold: 1968**

Number of Persons in Household	Income
One	$1,748
Two	2,262
Three	2,774
Four	3,553
Five	4,188
Six	4,706
Seven	5,789

involved. Nevertheless, very large differentials still provide meaningful insights. The threshold income shown in Table 1 for a four-person household is equivalent to an annual per capita income of $853 in 1967 dollars. In that year, per capita national income in nations containing over one-third of the

free world's total population was *under* *$100.*[5] Thus, many
"poor" Americans would be considered wealthy by a large
portion of the world.

    But whether people *feel* poor or not depends to some
extent on how their incomes compare with the incomes of
other people around them. On this basis, U.S. poverty income
thresholds are extremely low. A Bureau of Labor Statistics
study in 1967 indicated that achieving a *moderate* standard of
living for a family of two adults and two children would cost
about $9,361 (in 1968 dollars) in the average metropolitan
area.[6] This "moderate income" standard is just about three
times as large as the poverty income threshold for a four-
person household in 1968. Similarly, a study conducted by
Real Estate Research Corporation in 1968 showed that using
the cost of housing, rather than the cost of food, to define
poverty resulted in much higher income thresholds than those
set forth above.[7] Raising these thresholds would greatly increase
the number of persons considered poor in each of the categories
mentioned above. Therefore, the statistics presented in this
paper concerning the extent of urban poverty should be regarded
as relatively low estimates which understate the number of
persons whom we ought to consider as poor by U.S. standards.
Yet we have been compelled to use these statistics because they
are by far the most accurate and comprehensive available.

    Thus, in this paper, any household with an annual income
less than the poverty income threshold appropriate to its size is
considered "in poverty." Other aspects of poverty more closely
related to income-earning capability will be discussed in the
analysis of each of the main categories of poor persons mentioned earlier.

    The definition of poverty described above has been widely
criticized by well-informed urban analysts. Three main objec-
tions to it have been advanced.

    It sets the "poverty level" too low. As noted earlier, this
level equals only about one-third of the estimated "moderate
standard of living" recently calculated by the BLS.

It is too static, because it fails to allow for the fact that society's concept of the "minimum standard of living" changes over time.[8] Items once viewed as luxuries frequently become widely distributed and are then considered "necessities." Examples are television sets and automobiles. Therefore, this view considers it improper to define any once-and-for-all "poverty line" based upon the cost of some fixed bundle of goods and services periodically adjusted to account for price changes. Rather, the "minimum bundle" should itself be gradually expanded over time as standards of living rise.

It fails to take into account the over-all distribution of incomes in society. This criticism contends that the level of satisfaction among poor people in modern society depends mainly upon how their incomes are related to those of others. Thus, even if everyone in society enjoys a significantly rising real income, the poor will still believe they are becoming worse off if the real incomes of the rest of society are rising faster than their own. They will consider their condition as improving only if the basic income distribution is altering to give them a larger share and someone else a lesser one. Since the entire income structure in the United States is rising absolutely, this relative view of poverty also requires a dynamic definition of the poverty level, rather than the static one used in this paper.

Replacing the Current Definition

Undoubtedly, each of these criticisms has some merit. However, insofar as this paper is concerned, that merit is not sufficient to overcome the lack of data about any definitions other than the one used here. But as the following facts indicate, an eventual replacement of that definition should be considered.

1. *Accepted definitions of the minimum standard of living have risen over time.* One of the first serious students of poverty in the United States used a figure of $460 as the "poverty line"

in 1904.[9] Correcting for price-level changes, that figure would equal about $1,787 in 1968 dollars. In 1950, an annual income of $2,000 for a four-person household was used as the poverty line by the Joint Economic Committee of Congress. That would equal about $2,893 in 1968 dollars. The poverty level actually in use in 1968 was $3,553.

However, official versions of the acceptable "minimum" have not increased as fast as real income. From 1950 to 1968 per capita disposable personal income (1958 prices) rose from $1,646 to $2,474 or 50.3 per cent. The "poverty level" (1968 prices) rose from $2,893 to $3,553 or 22.3 per cent. Thus, even if the poverty level is defined as gradually rising, it probably should be designed to rise more slowly than real income in general.

2.   *There has been very little change in U.S. income distribution for almost twenty years.*[10] From 1938 to 1947, equality in the United States increased significantly. But since 1947, the shares of total income received by the lowest fifth of all families and unrelated individuals have remained nearly constant.

Table 2. **Changes in Income Distribution: 1947–1968**

Type and Rank of Receiving Unit	Percentage of Aggregate Income (before federal taxes) Received by Each Group		
	1947	1950	1968
Families			
Lowest 20 per cent	5.0%	4.5%	5.7%
Highest 20 per cent	43.0	42.6	40.6
Highest 5 per cent	17.2	17.0	14.0
Unrelated Individuals			
Lowest 20 per cent	1.9	2.3	3.2
Highest 20 per cent	59.4	50.4	50.8
Highest 5 per cent	33.3	19.3	20.4

These figures show a decline in the share going to the top 20 per cent, but not much change in the share going to the lowest 20 per cent. Therefore, *from a purely relative point of view, there has been no decline in poverty whatsoever in the past twenty years.* Yet this conclusion is sharply at variance with conclusions based upon either increases in real income or the definition of poverty used in this paper. In the author's opinion, it is inappropriate to define poverty in completely relative terms. Rather, the relative-poverty argument can add support to the use of a dynamic measure that embodies a poverty level that rises over time but is not entirely relative.

3. *Transfer payments in the United States do reduce absolute poverty significantly.* A recent study using data for 1965 shows that public transfer payments—Social Security benefits, welfare payments, veterans benefits, unemployment compensation, and so forth—caused about 24 per cent of all households receiving transfer payments of any kind in that year (counting an unrelated individual as well as a family as a household) to rise above the poverty level.[11]

There were 10.8 million poor households *before* transfers; 4.7 million were made "nonpoor" by transfers; and 6.1 million remained in poverty even after receiving transfers. Public transfers thus removed 4.7 million households from poverty that year and reduced the number of households in poverty among the recipient households from 55 per cent to 31 per cent. These data indicate that significant income redistribution is occurring.

4. *The "poverty gap" derived from the Social Security Administration definition of poverty could be largely eliminated in the United States with only a modest change in the distribution of incomes.* That gap has been estimated at $9.85 billion in 1968. This amount is considerably smaller than the *annual increase* in federal tax receipts expected to occur in the near future without any rise in tax rates, simply because of the interaction of economic growth and inflation with the progressive federal rate structure. Hence, if only part of that "fiscal dividend" were devoted to attacking poverty in the next few

years by means of larger transfer payments, the entire poverty gap could be eliminated without raising tax rates.

It is true that this policy would result in some income redistribution. After all, the fiscal dividend could alternatively be used to cut taxes or for other government activities benefiting all income groups; and the claims made under the existing or planned programs already appear as large as the dividend anticipated for some years to come. For our present purpose, however, it will be assumed that an adequate portion of the fiscal dividend is made available for eliminating the poverty gap. Disposable personal income in 1970 will total about $645 billion in 1968 prices. So only about 1.5 per cent of the total disposable personal income would have to be transferred (in addition to that already being transferred) to eliminate the poverty gap.[12] Since the 5.0 million families and the 4.7 million unrelated individuals who were counted as "poor" in 1968 would presumably receive the 1.5 per cent (in addition to about 3.0 per cent of the nation's aggregate income they receive now), the remaining "nonpoor" would have to provide it out of their 97 per cent of the aggregate income. Each "nonpoor" household would have to sacrifice, on the average, about 1.6 per cent of its 1970 share—less than the likely growth from year to year. Hence, such a redistribution could be accomplished if each nonpoor household was willing to sacrifice about one-half of its expected annual gain in income. Of course, eliminating the poverty gap based on other definitions of poverty might require considerably larger redistributions.

3. The Extent of Urban Poverty[13]

In 1968, there were 25.4 million persons living in poverty in the entire United States—or 12.8 per cent of the total population. Of these persons, 17.4 million (69 per cent) were white, and 8.0 million (31 per cent) were nonwhite. Thus, there were twice as many poor whites as poor nonwhites. But the *incidence* of poverty (the probability of being poor) was 10.0 per cent for all whites, as compared to 33.5 per cent for all nonwhites.

The 212 metropolitan areas of the United States contained approximately 128.1 million people in 1968 or 65 per cent of the nation's total population.[14] Slightly more than half of all metropolitan area residents (70.1 million) lived in suburbs; the remainder (58.0 million) lived in central cities. About 12.9 million poor persons lived in these metropolitan areas, or 51 per cent of all U.S. poor. Thus, metropolitan areas as a whole contained a less-than-proportional share of poor persons. But within those areas, the proportion of poor in central cities was almost double that in the suburbs. Both the proportions and the numbers of poor persons, inside and outside metropolitan areas, are shown for 1968 in Table 3. Thus, central cities contain a higher proportion of poor persons than the nation as a whole, though a lower proportion than any nonmetropolitan areas. In contrast, suburbs contain a substantially smaller proportion of poverty than any other part of the nation.

Within metropolitan areas, the number of poor persons and the incidence of poverty for whites and nonwhites are shown in Table 4. These figures indicate that the incidence of poverty is higher in central cities than in suburbs for whites but the reverse for nonwhites.

Table 3. **Poverty in Metropolitan and Nonmetropolitan Areas: 1968**

Area	Number of Poor Persons (*Millions*)[a]	Percentage of Persons in Poverty
United States	25.4	12.8%
Metropolitan Areas	12.9	10.0
Central cities	7.8	13.4
Suburbs	5.1	7.3
Nonmetropolitan Areas	12.5	18.0
Nonfarm[b]	10.4	17.2
Farm[b]	2.2	23.5

a. Numerical subtotals may not add to totals because of rounding.
b. Estimates.

Table 4. **Poverty Among Whites and Nonwhites: 1968**

Area	Poor Whites		Poor Nonwhites	
	Number (*Millions*)	As a Percentage of All Whites	Number (*Millions*)	As a Percentage of All Nonwhites
Metropolitan Areas	8.5	7.6%	4.4	25.7%
Central cities	4.4	9.8	3.4	25.5
Suburbs	4.1	6.2	1.0	26.0

These figures also indicate that about 57 per cent of the 7.8 million poor persons living in central cities are white, and about 43 per cent are nonwhite. In contrast, about 80 per cent of the 5.1 million poor suburbanites are white, and only 20 per cent are nonwhite. Further, about 60 per cent of all the 12.9 million poor persons in metropolitan areas live in central cities.

Another conclusion implicit in Table 4 is that racial segregation in the suburbs does not result solely, or even mainly, from economic class discrimination. Poor white people are not excluded from suburban areas as a group, since 48 per cent of all poor whites in metropolitan areas in 1968 lived in the suburbs. In contrast, only 23 per cent of all poor nonwhites in metropolitan areas in 1968 lived in the suburbs. In fact, only

22 per cent of all *nonpoor* nonwhites lived in the suburbs—in contrast with 61 per cent of all nonpoor whites. Thus, the proportion of *poor whites* living in suburbs in 1968 was more than double the proportion of *nonpoor nonwhites* living there. This clearly indicates that it is not poverty that causes nonwhites to be excluded from suburban areas.

The record level of economic prosperity prevalent during the decade of the 1960's, plus various public policies designed to alleviate poverty, reduced markedly the total number of poor persons in the United States. According to the revised definition of poverty adopted in 1969,[15] there were 39.5 million poor persons in the nation during 1959. By 1968, this total had dropped by 14.1 million (or 36 per cent) to 25.4 million. At the same time, the percentage of persons below the poverty level (the incidence of poverty) decreased from 22.0 per cent in 1959 to 12.8 per cent in 1968 (or by 42 per cent). Since the total population in the United States rose during these nine years, the absolute decline in the *number* of poor persons resulted in an even greater reduction in the *proportion* of those in poverty. Nevertheless, these poor persons, numbering 25.4 million in 1968, still exceeded the entire population of Canada or about equalled half the population of France or the United Kingdom.

During the same period, the number of poor persons living in metropolitan areas declined by about 4.1 million (or 24 per cent), from 17.0 million to 12.9 million. The proportion of the poor, on the other hand, decreased from 15.3 per cent in 1959 to 10.0 per cent in 1968—by about one-third. Apparently, the number and proportion of persons in poverty declined more sharply outside metropolitan areas than within metropolitan areas. The migration of rural poor to the nation's urban centers and a larger population increase in these areas resulted in a smaller percentage decline in the metropolitan poor.

However, this reduction of poor persons in metropolitan areas was not experienced to an equal degree by all segments of its population. The number of whites below the poverty level decreased more rapidly than that of nonwhites. The number of poor whites decreased by 28 per cent between 1959 and 1968, from 11.8 million to 8.5 million. But the number of nonwhites in poverty fell only 15 per cent, from 5.2 million to 4.4 million. This disparity resulted partly from much faster population growth among nonwhites. The percentages of persons below the poverty line, on the other hand, declined by about one-third for both whites (from 12.0 per cent in 1959 to 7.6 per cent in 1968) and nonwhites (from 40.9 per cent to 25.7 per cent). Nevertheless, the poverty rate among nonwhites is still more than three times that among whites.

Trends of poverty among the metropolitan populations varied more markedly, depending upon the sex of household heads. The decrease in the number of poor persons over the last nine years has taken place primarily among households headed by a male. The number of poor persons living in such households declined nearly half between 1959 and 1968 for both whites and nonwhites. In contrast, those in households headed by a female increased by 9 per cent for whites and by 48 per cent for nonwhites. This is shown in Table 5.

Table 5. **Change in the Number of Poor Persons in Metropolitan Areas by Sex of Household Heads: 1959-1968**

	In All Households	With a Male Head	With a Female Head
(Millions)			
All Races	− 4.1	− 5.3	+ 1.2
White	− 3.4	− 3.7	+ 0.3
Nonwhite	− 0.8	− 1.6	+ 0.8
(Percentage change)			
All Races	−24.4%	−45.3%	+21.9%
White	−28.3	−44.2	+ 9.0
Nonwhite	−15.3	−47.9	+47.8

Because of these contrasting trends, the proportion of poor persons living in households headed by females rose to 50 per cent of the total metropolitan poor in 1968 from only 31 per cent in 1959. (Most of this increase in the number of poor persons in households headed by females was represented by children under eighteen years of age, as will be explained more fully in another section). Thus, the over-all decline of poverty population in metropolitan areas was not shared equally by poor households headed by men and those headed by women.

The increasing number of the poor among households headed by a female, combined with a large decline in such persons among households with a male head, caused a significant change in the characteristics of metropolitan poor. A greater portion of the metropolitan poor today is made up of those who are less equipped to take advantage of expanding employment opportunities and higher earnings enjoyed by general population in these areas.

Insomuch

Inasmuch

4. Specific Types of Urban Poverty

The 12.9 million poor persons in all U.S. metropolitan areas in 1968 can be divided into six major groups for purposes of analysis. Using the best available information, and supplementing it with some extrapolation and interpolation where necessary, we have developed estimates for 1968 which are shown in Table 6. These six groups have been defined so that there is no overlapping. Thus, all aged persons have been statistically separated as a group from their households; data on all children under eighteen are presented both separately and combined with those on the adults in their households. Compared to the aggregate data for all metropolitan areas, the percentage breakdowns for central cities and suburbs are less accurate; hence the former should be preferred as a basis for inference. However, the numerical and percentage breakdowns for the metropolitan area as a whole lead to the following significant conclusions.

The largest group of poor persons in metropolitan areas consists of children under eighteen. The 5.4 million such children constitute 42.2 per cent of all poor persons in these areas. This is about the same as the proportion of children in the total number of poor for the United States as a whole.

The second largest group of the metropolitan-area poor consists of elderly persons (sixty-five or over). The 2.4 million persons in this group make up 18.3 per cent of all such poor.

The third largest group is composed of adults in households headed by a female under sixty-five. The 2.3 million adults representing this group accounted for 17.6 per cent of all metro-

18

politan poor in 1968. If children in these households are included, the total number rises to 5.1 million, or 39.8 per cent of all metropolitan poor. *The most dramatic change that occurred in the composition of metropolitan poor has been an increase in the number of poor persons in households headed by a female.* While poor persons in households with a male head declined nearly half between 1959 and 1968, those in households with a female head (of all ages) increased by 22 per cent in the same period. In 1968, half of all metropolitan poor were living in households headed by a woman.

The fourth largest group is comprised of adults in households headed by a man who is regularly employed but earns a very low income. The adults in these households total 1.5 million persons, or 11.9 per cent of all metropolitan poor. If children under eighteen in these households are included, then the total number of persons is 3.2 million, or about one-fourth of all poor persons in metropolitan areas. Furthermore, some of the female-headed households in poverty also have employed heads with low incomes. Thus, *the poverty of about one-third of all poor persons in metropolitan areas stems from low earnings, rather than unemployment, underemployment, or inability to work caused by disability or old age.* Moreover, low-wage jobs are probably responsible for at least twice as much poverty in metropolitan areas as is unemployment.

The following sections deal with each of the six categories of urban poverty as defined in Table 6.

The Elderly Poor

In 1968, 2.4 million persons sixty-five years of age and over in metropolitan areas lived in poverty. They accounted for 20 per cent of all elderly persons in these areas, and 18 per cent of the total metropolitan poor.

Although one out of every five elderly persons in metropolitan areas was poor in 1968, this poverty incidence is much lower than the corresponding poverty rate in other parts of the

Table 6. **Breakdown of Poor People in Metropolitan Areas: 1968**

Population Group	Metropolitan Areas (Thou- sands)	(% of total)	Central Cities (Thou- sands)	(% of total)	Suburbs (Thou- sands)	(% of total)
Elderly (sixty-five and over)	2,353	18.3%	1,405	18.1%	948	18.5%
Children (under eighteen)	5,433	42.2	3,315	42.8	2,118	41.4
Adults in female- headed households (eighteen to sixty-four)	2,262	17.6	1,467	18.9	796	15.6
Adults in households headed by disabled males (eighteen to sixty-four)	392	3.0	219	2.8	173	3.4
Adults in households headed by unemployed males (eighteen to sixty-four)*	903	7.0	553	7.1	346	6.7
Adults in households headed by employed males (eighteen to sixty-four)	1,528	11.9	795	10.3	736	14.4
All persons in poverty	12,871	100.0	7,754	100.0	5,117	100.0

*This group represents the households headed by males who were either unemployed or worked less than 40 weeks a year.

nation. The proportions of elderly persons below the poverty line by type of residence during 1968 are shown in Table 7.

Table 7. **Proportion of Elderly Persons in Poverty: 1968**

Area	All Elderly	White Elderly	Nonwhite Elderly
United States	25.0%	23.1%	46.6%
Metropolitan Areas	20.0	19.3	35.0
Central cities	22.3	20.9	33.9
Suburbs	18.3	17.4	38.9
Nonmetropolitan Areas	32.3	29.3	64.5
Nonfarm*	31.8	29.1	62.5
Farm*	35.1	31.0	76.1

*Estimates based on the number of poor families headed by persons 65 years of age and over.

As in other parts of the United States, the proportion of elderly persons living in poverty was much higher among nonwhites than among whites in all metropolitan areas. But the nonwhite population in metropolitan areas is much younger than the white population on the average. Therefore, nonwhites make up a relatively small fraction (13 per cent in 1968) of all elderly poor in these areas. Within metropolitan areas, the percentage of aged persons in poverty was only slightly higher in central cities (22.3 per cent) than in suburbs (18.3 per cent).

LIKELY CAUSES OF THEIR POVERTY. Poverty is more prevalent among the elderly part of the U.S. population than any other age group. There are several probable causes of this situation.

Compulsory retirement, voluntary retirement, and decreased working capabilities cause a high proportion of persons sixty-five and over to stop working, thereby drastically cutting their incomes. Many aged persons *became poor* when they stopped working and no longer earned incomes. The annual consumer income survey conducted by the Bureau of the Census showed that approximately 57 per cent of the nation's aged couples and 76 per cent of all elderly individuals had no *earned* income in 1968.[16]

The definition of poverty upon which almost all statistical analyses are based is centered upon the annual *money income* reported by the households or individuals concerned. However, many aged persons who are retired have low incomes which they supplement by drawing upon accumulated savings, or making use of assets which provide benefits not counted as income (such as owner-occupied homes that are fully paid for). Thus, use of money income alone as a measure of the economic well-being of the elderly is likely to understate their condition somewhat and to categorize as "poor" many persons who are reasonably well off. A similar distortion is caused by under-reporting of income by older persons in order to avoid reductions in their Social Security benefits.

It is not possible to estimate accurately the extent to which these distortions occur. However, the median size of assets for couples sixty-five and over in 1962 was $11,180 including value of home, but only $2,950 excluding that value.[17] For elderly unmarried men and women, median asset holdings were under $3,300, including home values. About one-sixth of all elderly couples and two-fifths of unmarried elderly men and women had either no assets at all, or less than $1,000 in assets. Another one-fourth of all elderly couples and two-fifths of elderly individuals had no assets other than the value of their homes. Hence, assets do not make up for low incomes for a great many elderly people.

Moreover, it should be remembered that the poverty threshold incomes for two-person households and individuals are extremely low. Therefore, the error caused by ignoring assets may be more than offset by the opposite one of concluding that anyone with an income just barely larger than these thresholds does not suffer from the ill effects of poverty.

Not all elderly persons receive benefits from public or private retirement programs. If those who do not receive such benefits have no other significant resources, they are compelled to live in poverty. Even though 90 per cent of all persons now employed are covered by Federal Old Age Survivors, Disability, and Health Insurance (OASDHI) and related programs, a much lower proportion of persons now sixty-five and over were so covered when they were working. Currently, about 15 per cent of all elderly persons sixty-five and over do not receive any benefit payments from the OASDHI program.[18]

The level of payment under most retirement programs is not sufficient in itself to raise the recipients out of poverty. The average benefit payment for retired workers under the OASDHI program was about $1,186 in 1968, for their wives and husbands it was $615, and for their children it was $460.[19] These amounts are far below the poverty threshold applicable for the equivalent household size. It was estimated that about one-third of all aged households receiving benefit payments from this program in 1965 were in poverty, though about two-thirds would have been so without the benefit payments in that year.[20] It is true that many recipients of OASDHI benefits also have other sources of income. But these other sources are not very large either.

POVERTY TRENDS AMONG THE ELDERLY. Trend data for elderly poor in metropolitan areas are not available. However, it is reasonable to assume that recent trends operative for the nation's elderly as a whole are probably equally prevalent in metropolitan areas. The proportion of persons sixty-five and over living in poverty declined significantly from 1959 to 1968 for almost every group, as shown in Table 8.

The only group which experienced very little decline in the proportion of poor consisted of nonwhite, unrelated individuals sixty-five and over. Nevertheless, nearly half of all elderly unrelated individuals and almost one-fifth of all families with an aged head still lived in poverty in 1968.

Another important fact relevant to changes in elderly poverty over a period of time is the availability in the past few years of Medicare assistance, which has reduced substantially the cost of medical help for the aged.

Table 8. **Breakdown of Households with Elderly Heads:
1959 and 1968**

Type of Household	Percentage of Such Households in Poverty	
	1959	1968
Families		
Total	30.0%	17.0%
White	26.8	15.1
Nonwhite	70.9	39.0
Male Head	29.7	15.9
Female Head	31.5	22.3
Unrelated Individuals		
Total	66.0	48.8
White	65.0	46.7
Nonwhite	76.6	70.2
Male	58.5	43.5
Female	69.1	50.6

SIGNIFICANT RESULTS OF SUCH POVERTY. The main result of poverty among the elderly is the low quality of life in which many of them are compelled to live. They must watch every penny carefully, cannot indulge in much entertainment or recreation, are often terribly lonely because they cannot afford to visit others or "keep up appearances" at home, must live in small and minimum-quality housing, and frequently cannot afford adequate medical care. As a result, in a society which separates the elderly from other more active members (such as younger families with children), many elderly poor live extremely restricted and barren lives with minimal human contact. This result, rather than any loss of potential production or other impact upon the economy as a whole, is the most significant consequence of poverty among older people.

Poor Children Under Eighteen

In 1968, about 5.4 million children under eighteen lived in poverty in metropolitan areas. They constituted 12.2 per cent of all children under eighteen living in those areas, and 42.2

per cent of the total metropolitan poor in that year. Of the 5.4 million poor children, about 54 per cent (3.0 million) were whites, and the remaining 46 per cent (2.5 million) were nonwhites. Also, nearly two-thirds of all metropolitan poor children lived in central cities.

The incidence of poverty for children was twice as high in central cities as in suburbs. The poverty rates for children by type of residence as well as by race are shown in the table below.

There was a large disparity between whites and nonwhites in the proportions of children who were poor. The percentage of poor among nonwhite children living in metropolitan areas (33.5 per cent) was about four times as high as that among white children (7.9 per cent). Among nonwhite children who were poor, about three-fourths lived in central cities, and the remaining one-fourth lived in suburban rings. As a result of this concentration of poor children in central cities and of larger family sizes among nonwhites, about 56 per cent of all poor children in central cities were nonwhites, although the total nonwhite children constituted only 30 per cent of all children living in those cities in 1968.

It should be noted, however, that the proportion of poor among nonwhite children was significantly lower in metropolitan areas than in other parts of the nation. The figures in the table below show the overwhelming preponderance of poverty among nonwhite children outside metropolitan areas. It is easy

Table 9. **Proportion of Children Under Eighteen in Poverty: 1968**

Area	All Races	White	Nonwhites
United States	15.3%	10.7%	41.6%
Metropolitan Areas	12.2	7.9	33.5
Central cities	17.6	11.0	33.5
Suburbs	8.2	6.3	33.4
Nonmetropolitan Areas	20.9	15.4	58.4
Nonfarm	19.3	14.2	55.1
Farm	33.6	25.4	79.7

to understand why so many nonwhite parents have moved their families to metropolitan areas in the hope of finding better conditions.

The poverty status of children is closely associated with the presence or absence of a father. In 1968, the poverty rate for children who were living in families headed by women (53.6 per cent) was eight times as high as that for children living in families with a male head (6.5 per cent) in all metropolitan areas. This is shown in Table 10 below.

Table 10. **Impoverished Children in Families Classified by Sex of Family Head: 1968**

	Male Head			Female Head		
	All Races	White	Non-whites	All Races	White	Non-whites
Metropolitan Areas	6.5%	4.9%	17.4%	53.6%	41.8%	69.3%
Central cities	8.8	6.5	16.2	57.9	45.6	67.8
Suburbs	5.1	4.1	20.7	46.2	38.0	75.9

In 1968, more than half of all poor children in metropolitan areas were living with families headed by a woman. These children without a father were predominantly in central cities (more than two-thirds of all such children).

Poverty among children is also highly correlated with the size of their families. The more children there are in a family, the higher the probability that it is poor. This is shown in Table 11 for the entire United States.

As a result, a high proportion of these poor children were in families with a large number of children. In 1968, about 44 per cent of all U.S. poor children were living in families with five or more children. If the presence of four or more children is used as a cutoff point, this proportion becomes 62 per cent. Thus, nearly two-thirds of all poor children in the United States were in families with four or more children. The percentage of poor children living in large families was even higher among nonwhite families and families with female heads. These figures are for the United States as a whole, but it is reasonable to assume similar relationships between poverty and family size within metropolitan areas.

Table 11. **Impoverished Children Under Eighteen by Size of Family: 1968**

Number of Children in Family	Percentage of Families in Poverty		
	White	Nonwhite	All
None	7.3%	16.8%	8.0%
One	6.3	20.9	7.9
Two	6.1	26.8	8.1
Three	9.1	34.0	11.8
Four	11.6	41.9	16.0
Five	21.5	50.2	27.5
Six or more	23.3	58.4	34.4

LIKELY CAUSES OF THEIR POVERTY. Our analysis has broken down all households into five groups, as explained previously. Through a complex process of estimation, we have distributed all 5.4 million poor children in metropolitan areas among four of these five groups (arbitrarily assuming that elderly households contain no children under eighteen). The results of this distribution are shown in Table 12.[21] The specific causes of poverty in each group of households containing children are discussed later.

POVERTY TRENDS AMONG CHILDREN UNDER EIGHTEEN. Between 1959 and 1968, the number of poor children in metropolitan areas declined from 6.3 million to 5.4 million, with a higher proportionate decrease occurring among whites than among nonwhites. The number of poor white children decreased by 28 per cent during this period (from 4.1 million to 3.0 million), whereas the number of poor nonwhite children decreased only by 6 per cent (from 2.6 million to 2.5 million). As a result, the proportion of nonwhites among the total number

of poor children rose to 46 per cent in 1968 from 39 per cent
in 1959.

Table 12. **Persons in Poverty by Type of Household
in All Metropolitan Areas: 1968**

Type of Household	Adults	Children *(Thousands)*	Total	Percentage of Total
Headed by females under 65	2,262	2,855	5,117	39.8%
Headed by disabled males under 65	392	192	584	4.5
Headed by unemployed males under 65	903	755	1,658	12.9
Headed by employed males under 65	1,528	1,631	3,159	24.5
Headed by persons 65 or over	2,353	—	2,353	18.3
ALL PERSONS	7,437	5,433	12,871	100.0

Table 13. **Change in the Number of Poor Children in Urban
Areas by Sex of Family Head: 1959–1968**

	In All Families	With a Male Head	With a Female Head
(Millions)			
All Races	− 1.3	− 2.3	+ 1.0
White	− 1.2	− 1.5	+ 0.3
Nonwhite	− 0.1	− 0.8	+ 0.7
(Percentage change)			
All Races	−19.6%	−47.6%	+55.6%
White	−28.4	−47.4	+38.0
Nonwhite	− 5.7	−48.0	+73.2

The sex of family heads made a more significant difference
than race in poverty trends among children. The reduction in
the number of poor children that occurred in metropolitan
areas during this period was entirely among families headed by
a male. As shown above, however, poor children living in

families headed by females increased by 38 per cent among whites and by 73 per cent among nonwhites.

Although the number of poor children in families headed by a female rose during this period, the percentage of children in poverty decreased in all types of families. The proportion of poor among children who were in families with a male head dropped from 13.8 per cent in 1959 to 6.5 per cent in 1968. But for children living in families headed by a woman, the poverty rate decreased only slightly, from 57.4 per cent to 53.6 per cent. In terms of race, the poverty rate for white children fell from 12.2 per cent to 7.9 per cent; for nonwhite children, from 50.4 per cent to 33.5 per cent. Thus, the proportionate decline in the incidence of poverty was greater for children who lived in families with a male head than for those in families without a male head, and greater for white children than for nonwhites. In spite of some decline in recent years, however, poverty has been persistent, especially among children living in nonwhite, female-headed families. They were still subject to a very high poverty rate—69.3 per cent in 1968.

SIGNIFICANT RESULTS OF SUCH POVERTY. Poverty experienced by children has several important impacts—all bad. Several of the more serious consequences are discussed below.

Really severe poverty frequently causes *lack of adequate food and properly balanced diets.* According to a food consumption survey conducted by the Department of Agriculture in 1965, about 63 per cent of households with incomes under $3,000 in that year had inadequate diets.[22] Recent research shows that such deprivation may inhibit the growth of the brain, especially during the first few years of life, thus retarding a child's mental capacities. This clearly affects a child's ability to escape from poverty once he grows up.[23] Certainly not all poor children in the United States have inadequate diets. But recent research shows that many do.

The cultural and psychological atmosphere in many poor households *impairs the development among children of feelings of security and belonging*, as well as their capacity to absorb education successfully. Poor families are inherently under strong economic strains. Also, they often suffer from other fundamental disabilities related to their low capacity to earn income. For example, one of the adults may be alcoholic, or have very low verbal and other skills, or suffer from some acute neurosis. Moreover, poor families are less able to obtain help in ameliorating such conditions than middle-class families; they cannot afford such help and are less likely to understand how to use social institutions to obtain it free. As a result, a home atmosphere of tension and conflict often impairs poor children's emotional stability or their ability to absorb formal education in school. Furthermore, the common failure of poor adults to read books or newspapers, or even to carry on sustained conversations, provides very weak educational preparation for many poor children. Consequently, when they enter school, they are less able to learn basic reading, writing, mathematical, and social skills than children from families with greater advantages. So school often confronts poor children with personal failure. This reinforces the feelings of inferiority and lack of capability they may already sense by comparing their dress, possessions, and speech with those of children they see in school and on television. Hence many poor children fall farther and farther behind in school, and generally fail to develop the basic skills necessary to break out of poverty in our education-oriented society, whether they actually drop out of school or not.[24]

Some recent evidence indicates that the particular way mothers handle and talk to their infants *may affect the mental capacities of children at later stages of life.*[25] The greater the tactile, visual, and auditory stimulation provided to tiny babies, the more alert they become, and the faster they can learn reading and other basic skills. Children in poor households are less likely to receive such stimulation than those in wealthier homes because (1) poor households contain more children on the average, so the mother's attention is often diverted to other children; (2) many poor mothers must work and cannot spend much time with their infants, who are frequently left to relatives or baby-sitters; (3) lower-income mothers are less familiar with proper child-rearing techniques than wealthier mothers who consult with pediatricians regularly.

Many poor families with children need the earnings which those children can bring in at a relatively early age—such as in the late teens. Hence poverty *compels some children to drop out of high school to go to work,* and certainly prevents many intelligent children from poor families from going on to higher educational institutions.

These results not only reduce the quality of life experienced by the children concerned, but also have significant negative effects for society as a whole. First, they drastically reduce the contribution to society made by many poor children when they grow up. In fact, many become dependent upon public support. Second, these effects tend to be self-perpetuating in at least some cases. They prevent many persons reared in poverty from escaping it, and make it likely that the children of the poor will suffer from the same disabilities.

Poor Households Headed by Females

In 1968, there were 2.3 million adults under sixty-five years of age in households with poverty incomes headed by females in all metropolitan areas, and 2.9 million children under age eighteen also lived in such families, for a total of 5.1 million persons. This total comprised 39.8 per cent of all poor persons in metropolitan areas in that year. If the aged persons in these households are also included, the total rises to 6.5 million—slightly more than a half of all metropolitan poor in 1968. Whites constituted about 60 per cent of this total. More than two-thirds of poor households headed by women lived in central cities.

Leaving out unrelated individuals, about 86 per cent of all families headed by a female in metropolitan areas included children. Of all the population groups analyzed in this paper, these families headed by a female with dependent children had the highest incidence of poverty. The proportion in poverty among women heading a family with one or more children was 42.8 per cent in 1968 (33.5 per cent for white women and 60.1 per cent for nonwhite). In comparison, female heads of families without children registered a poverty rate of only 10.1 per cent. On the average, poor families headed by women had more children per family than families headed by a man.

Moreover, the poverty-proneness of families headed by women appears to be almost directly proportional to the number of children they have. Detailed statistics that illustrate the relationship between the incidence of poverty and the number of dependent children in a family are not available for metropolitan areas. However, national data may provide reasonably accurate information in this respect. This relationship is shown in Table 14 for the nation as a whole.

Table 14. **Percentage of Female-Headed Households in Poverty: 1968**

Number of Children	Total	White	Nonwhite
None	13.6%	12.3%	21.7%
One	29.8	25.1	43.7
Two	38.2	31.5	54.8
Three	55.7	50.4	66.5
Four	66.2	57.3	77.6
Five	73.8	63.9	81.5
Six or more	75.5	66.2	82.5
ALL	32.3	25.2	52.9

The close correlation between poverty and the number of dependent children is strikingly apparent from the doubling in proportion of families in poverty from those without children to those with one child. The ratio increases as the number of children rises.

Data on work experience of the female heads of families in poverty reveal another aspect of their poverty that is closely related to the presence of dependent children. As shown in Table 15, the majority of these women did not work during 1968 because of their responsibilities at home.

Table 15. **Distribution of Female Heads of Poor Families by Work Experience: 1968**

	United States	Metropolitan Areas
	(Percentage)	
Total	100.0%	100.0%
Did not work	56.0	58.6
Reason: Keeping house	43.6	(n.a.)
Other	12.4	(n.a.)
Worked 1 to 49 weeks	27.5	25.3
Worked 50 weeks or more	16.5	16.1

Thus, of all the poor women heading a family in metropolitan areas, only 16 per cent worked all year, 25 per cent worked part of the year, and the remaining 59 per cent did not work at all. It is believed that many of these poor mothers with young children are unable to work because of their child-care responsibilities.[26] Unless suitable child-care facilities are available, therefore, they cannot be expected to find any gainful employment outside their homes.

LIKELY CAUSES OF THEIR POVERTY. The most obvious cause of poverty in these households is the need of mothers to stay home and care for their children, which prevents them from working full-time, or at all. Furthermore, for those who are able to work, available jobs are mostly at the lower end of the pay scale. It is estimated that in the United States as a whole, about 36 per cent of all employed white women heading a poor family and 65 per cent of all such nonwhite women were in service occupations in 1968; one of the lowest paid groups.[27] It is, then, not hard to understand why a considerable number of poor women who wanted to work have instead chosen public assistance as "a more secure existence."[28] Although the data are generally sketchy, one government survey showed that about 70 per cent of mothers receiving Aid to Families with Dependent Children in 1966 could not earn more by working than they receive in public assistance payments because of their low skill and educational levels.[29]

Thus, the real source of poverty in such households consists of whatever causes them to be without male heads. These factors include death, divorce, desertion, and illegitimacy. The rate of illegitimacy has been rising sharply in recent years; among nonwhites, it was over 26 per cent nationally in 1966, and over 50 per cent in some low-income, central-city areas.[30]

The high proportion of female-headed families among all U.S. nonwhites (over 27 per cent in 1968 as compared to only 9 per cent among whites) has led some observers to conclude that a matriarchal culture has developed among low-income nonwhites, in which minimal responsibility is felt or exercised by fathers.[31] Some observers link this phenomenon with the historic breakup of Negro families under slavery. However, exactly the same phenomenon is found in the low-income urban parts of most Latin American nations. Yet in those nations, slavery insofar as it existed at all did not involve breaking up families. So it seems more likely that paternal irresponsibility results from either the inability of low-income, poorly-skilled men to obtain the kind of employment required to support a family, or from an inherent element in lower-income culture, or from some combination of these.[32] Thus, the "ultimate" cause of poverty among households headed by women may be the inability of a certain group of adult men to obtain steady, well-paying jobs, plus the cultural weakness of the family structure in low-income, urban societies. Since these two factors are closely related and probably mutually reinforcing, it is extremely difficult to decide to what degree each is responsible.

Another cause of poverty among the households headed by women is the low level of public assistance provided to support such households. In most states, the amounts furnished by public authorities are far below the poverty thresholds for the various family sizes concerned.[33] Moreover, the widespread practice of deducting a large part of earnings (above the first $30 a month) from the amount of public assistance discourages those members from accepting legitimate employment.[34] Yet, since public assistance is so low, they often need additional funds. Thus, "the system" encourages illegal activities such as prostitution, dope peddling, bootlegging, and gambling, since income so earned will not be reported to public-assistance authorities.

POVERTY TRENDS AMONG FEMALE-HEADED HOUSEHOLDS. In contrast to the generally declining trend in the number of poor in metropolitan areas, poor persons living in households headed by a female (of all ages) increased by 22 per cent from 5.3 million in 1959 to 6.5 million in 1968. The rate of increase was greater among nonwhites than among whites. The number of poor nonwhites living in households of this type increased by 48 per cent from 1.8 million to 2.6 million, whereas whites increased by 9 per cent from 3.5 million to 3.8 million. As stated previously, most of this increase was accounted for by children under eighteen years of age. The number of poor children in these households increased by 56 per cent from 1.8 million in 1959 to 2.9 million in 1968.

Although the *number* of poor persons in these households rose between 1959 and 1968, the *proportion* of such persons in poverty slightly decreased for both whites and nonwhites. Among whites, the proportion dropped from 29.8 per cent in 1959 to 28.8 per cent in 1968; among nonwhites, from 62.5 per cent to 54.8 per cent. Obviously, the incidence of poverty declined more slowly for persons in households with a female head than for those in households with a male head in this period.

SIGNIFICANT RESULTS OF SUCH POVERTY. Children growing up in fatherless households suffer a serious psychological and emotional handicap, regardless of their economic problems, because they lack a father-model. This is particularly true of boys. They have no authority figure to assist them in learning to deal with the outside world, and to provide a role-model after which to pattern their own behavior. Poverty tends to aggravate the negative results of such a situation. It adds to the tensions within the family, and often forces the mother to work part-time or full-time—further reducing the concerned supervision received by the children. Moreover, poverty may be responsible for the absence of a father in the household, insofar as it undermines the willingness of fathers to remain present when they have clearly failed to perform the role of adequate family supporter.

To the extent that poverty compels mothers to reduce supervision of their children because they must work, or cannot afford living in areas where supervised play is possible, it tends to encourage the development of relatively undisciplined children. Many of these children grow up almost spontaneously "on the street" in a vicious atmosphere of cynicism and exploitation, without any exposure to the basic values of American society and culture. These children are responsible for a very high proportion of urban crime and for starting many of the recent civil disorders in our cities. Therefore, poverty in such households has extremely significant detrimental results, particularly in our larger cities.

Poor Households Headed by Disabled Males Under Sixty-five

We have estimated that about 392,000 poor adults were in households headed by disabled males under sixty-five in all metropolitan areas in 1968. These households also contained about 192,000 children under eighteen or a total of 584,000 persons. This total accounted for 4.5 per cent of all poor persons in metropolitan areas in 1968.

For the nation as a whole the proportion in poverty among families headed by a male who did not work because of illness or disability was 36.2 per cent in 1968. This included such families with male heads sixty-five years old and over, among whom 35.1 per cent were poor. The corresponding percentage for families with disabled male heads under age sixty-five was 37.1 per cent.

The obvious cause of poverty among such households is a combination of inability to work due to illness or disability, and the relatively low level of whatever public assistance or compensation payments were received during the period of non-employment.

Poverty makes it harder for disabled or sick people to recover their income-earning capacity by procuring medical or other assistance, especially if such assistance is expensive. Hence, it tends to perpetuate itself by prolonging the particular illness or disability.

Children reared in homes where poverty exists because of disability or illness may suffer from some of the effects described in the discussion of poverty among children under eighteen. However, if the disability or illness has hit a family with a stable structure, a strong positive orientation toward education, and considerable educational and other cultural experience among its adult members, the effects of poverty may be much less severe than in households that are poor for other reasons.

Poor Households Headed by Non-disabled but Unemployed Males Under Sixty-five

The creation of new jobs for men is often cited as the most effective possible cure for urban poverty. However, only about one out of every eight poor persons in metropolitan areas (13.9 per cent) lived in households headed by either unemployed or underemployed males under sixty-five years of age in 1968. And nearly half of these persons were children.

In the United States as a whole, about 14.1 per cent of all families with unemployed male heads (of all ages) were in poverty in 1968. The proportion of poor among nonwhites (21.8 per cent) was almost twice that among whites (12.9 per cent). (For families with unemployed *female* heads, the proportions in poverty were 61.0 per cent among nonwhites and 39.9 per cent among whites). The Census Bureau also calculates poverty percentages among households in which there are "no earners." This category may include those where potential workers have ceased looking for work because of prolonged unemployment.

Clearly, the major cause of poverty in these households was unemployment. Therefore, a search for the "ultimate" causes would involve an analysis of why the male heads of these households were unemployed. Some of them were undoubtedly unemployed because of lack of any marketable skills or of the basic willingness to work hard. In many cases, these deficiencies were probably the results of prior poverty suffered during childhood. Thus, insofar as poverty inhibits the development of employment skills and proper education in young people, it tends to perpetuate itself by reducing their employment opportunities.

The poverty associated with unemployment has many of the negative impacts upon children discussed earlier. Moreover, failure of the male household-head to get a good job tends to discredit his capabilities as a provider in his own eyes and the eyes of his family. This creates feelings of self-deprecation, failure, and anxiety, which in turn may cause the male to flee the household, or at least to create unhealthy psychological tensions within it.[35] Hence, unemployment has a directly weakening effect upon family structure, particularly in low income areas with a tradition of fragmented family structure.

Poor Households Headed by Employed Males Under Sixty-five

In 1968, there were approximately 1.5 million adults and 1.6 million children, for a total of 3.2 million persons, living in poor households headed by a man under sixty-five who worked forty weeks or more during that year in all metropolitan areas.

This total comprised 24.5 per cent of all poor persons in metropolitan areas. As it is clear from the above description, this group represents both one-person households and family units headed by a regularly employed man under sixty-five.

Because of the data limitation, however, the following discussion on the incidence of poverty for this group covers only *heads of families*, including male heads sixty-five years and over, but does not cover unrelated individuals. The proportions of poor families with a regularly employed male head living in metropolitan areas in 1968 are shown in Table 16 below. In addition, the poverty rates among families with a male head who worked less than forty weeks during that year are also shown separately in this table.

Table 16. **Proportion of Families Headed by Employed Males Living in Poverty: 1968**

	Worked more than forty weeks	Worked less than forty weeks
	(Percentage)	
All families	2.4%	8.9%
White	1.9	7.3
Nonwhite	6.9	20.0

As shown in Table 16, the poverty proportion was much higher among nonwhite families than among white families. A higher poverty rate was also recorded for men who worked only part of the year than for those who worked year-round. However, the incidence of poverty among these employed male heads was much lower for the metropolitan areas than for the United States as a whole. For the nation as a whole, the percentage of poor among families with a year-round employed male head was 4.3 per cent in 1968, and 13.8 per cent among those with a male head who worked less than forty weeks. As described before, these figures refer to family heads only. Poverty among unrelated individuals would be undoubtedly much higher.

It is clear from the above information that *the vast majority of families headed by regularly employed males under sixty-five in metropolitan areas did not live in poverty.* Nevertheless, those who did live in poverty comprised almost one-fourth of all poor persons living in metropolitan areas.

LIKELY CAUSES OF THEIR POVERTY. Inadequate family incomes of the working poor results from *low wages, insufficient hours of work, large family size,* or a combination of these factors.

The minimum wage of $1.60 per hour currently in effect is equivalent to an annual income of $3,328 for someone who works forty hours per week, fifty-two weeks per year. If a family of four persons has only one earner, its family income at this minimum wage would still fall below the poverty level. Men who worked year-round but are paid less than this minimum wage, or those who receive the minimum wage but have a large family, would still remain in poverty. The Heineman Commission estimates that there are at least ten million jobs in the United States—including some state and municipal jobs—which pay less than the current federal minimum wage.[36]

Even relatively high-wage occupations often experience periodic layoffs during a typical year. (In fact, in the building trades, that is one reason why hourly rates are so high). Unskilled workers are likely to be the last hired and the first laid off. Since they earn the lowest wages, the sporadic nature of their work often reduces their total incomes below the poverty level.

The poorest-paid workers are usually those with the least skills and the least desirable work habits. Hence they may either get fired periodically, or voluntarily shift jobs because they are dissatisfied. This creates periods between jobs when they have no income.

These factors in turn have deeper causes. For example, low wages result primarily from the structure and job requirements of certain occupations, and from lack of skill among workers. These two factors are also related, since some occupations require relatively little skill and experience. Thus, the proportion of all employed family heads (of both sexes) who were in poverty varies sharply by occupation, as shown in Table 17. Within each type of job, the proportion of poverty among employed family heads is two to four times as high among nonwhites as among whites.

Some of the causes of lack of skill among workers are related to the impact of poverty upon children discussed earlier. Children from poor families have enormous handicaps in acquiring the education and training needed to obtain jobs in our technologically-oriented economy. Moreover, many unions in skilled trades have deliberate policies of holding down the number of new entrants so they can keep wages high—particularly if the newcomers are Negroes. This blocks many young people from acquiring skills through the apprenticeship career path.

Table 17. **Employed Family Heads Living in Poverty in the United States, by Occupation: 1968**

Occupation	All Families	White *(Percentage)*	Nonwhite
All occupations	6.7%	5.1%	21.9%
Professional & technical workers	1.8	1.5	6.8
Farmers & farm managers	22.6	20.4	62.4
Managers (except farm)	3.4	3.1	14.9
Clerical and sales workers	3.7	3.3	9.9
Craftsmen and foremen	3.7	3.2	12.1
Operatives	6.4	5.0	15.4
Private household workers	53.8	34.1	62.9
Other service workers	12.7	9.1	25.4
Nonfarm laborers	15.3	11.8	24.2
Farm laborers & foremen	37.9	29.7	62.5

POVERTY TRENDS AMONG EMPLOYED MALES UNDER SIXTY-FIVE. We were not able to obtain detailed information on recent trends concerning poverty in this group in metropolitan areas.

However, it is reasonable to assume that their poverty has been declining in roughly the same way as in the United States as a whole.

The number of poor families headed by a man who worked fifty weeks or more a year declined more than half between 1959 and 1968. At the same time, the proportion of such families in poverty dropped from 10.0 per cent in 1959 to 3.9 per cent in 1968. As might be expected, the incidence of poverty for families headed by a regularly employed male has been the lowest among all types of families. Although the poverty rate among nonwhite families of this type is still about four times as high as among white families, the proportionate decline in the poverty rate was greater for nonwhites (from 36.6 per cent in 1959 to 11.9 per cent in 1968) than for whites (from 8.1 per cent to 3.3 per cent). The number and proportion of poor families with a male head who worked less than a full year also declined in this period. *The decline in poverty during the last nine years has apparently taken place primarily among families headed by men who were working.*

SIGNIFICANT RESULTS OF SUCH POVERTY. Poverty among households with employed male heads under sixty-five has many of the same results previously described in relation to other types of poor households. There are, however, some major differences.

While children in such households do not suffer from the lack of a father, or from the father's complete inability to support his family, this presumed strength can produce some negative social consequences.

Insofar as the father works hard but fails to earn a good income, the respect of all family members—especially children— for the justice of the economic system or the value of legitimate employment may be eroded. It is hard to know how extensive or significant the resulting cynicism may be. But such cynicism is apparently one factor that leads many poor children to eschew middle-class values and to participate in destructive activities such as crime, vandalism, and rioting.

Inability of employed fathers to earn sufficient income to get a family out of poverty also creates a strong incentive for mothers to work. This may tend to reduce drastically the level of family supervision over children, and therefore weaken the family's ability to transmit key social and other values to them, as explained earlier. Moreover, this effect may persist even after the mother's additional earnings lift the family's income past the poverty level.

5. How Social Institutions Reinforce Poverty

For many poor people, poverty is not just a lack of income. It also involves a deprived and defeatist state of mind, a persistent lack of capability for improving one's own situation, and an inferior or dependent position in society. Moreover, major social institutions repeatedly reinforce these maladies—even when those institutions are specifically intended to alleviate poverty. In fact, almost every analysis of urban poverty has concluded that the system of institutions in which the poor are enmeshed tends to perpetuate their poverty. Consequently, attempts to eliminate poverty which provide direct aid to poor persons are bound to fail in the long run unless they also significantly alter the institutional systems surrounding the poor.

Social institutions reinforce poverty by:

Providing assistance to the poor in ways that increase or emphasize their dependency, rather than stimulating feelings of adequacy or efforts at self-improvement.

Exploiting the ignorance of the poor by imposing on them higher costs than other people pay for similar good or services.

Omitting poor people from social insurance schemes that "spread the risks" of certain social maladies and thereby lighten the burden of those maladies upon each household covered.

Creating unnecessary obstacles which prevent poor people from taking advantage of opportunities for improving their incomes, living conditions, or general capabilities.

Imposing middle-class standards and behavior patterns upon lower-class groups in a way that weakens the abilities of the latter to improve themselves in ways not morally acceptable to the middle class.

Measuring social services in terms of quantity-of-inputs rather than quality-of-outputs in determining "equality" of public service distribution among areas or social groups.

In this brief paper it is impossible to provide a detailed or comprehensive analysis of how social institutions reinforce poverty in all the ways set forth above. Instead, a few important examples have been summarized.

1.   Retail prices for food and other staples paid by residents of big-city, low-income neighborhoods are often higher than those paid by residents of higher-income areas. This occurs mainly because poor people tend to shop in small local stores, rather than because of price differentials in larger chain stores.[37]

2.   Poor residents of big cities pay much higher prices and interest rates for merchandise purchased on credit than wealthier residents pay for exactly the same goods. A Federal Trade Commission study showed that prices of such goods averaged 50 per cent higher in low-income areas.[38]

3.   Housing in low-income areas is far more expensive in relation to the quality of service received—especially in Negro areas—than in middle-income neighborhoods. For comparable or only slightly lower rents, poor households receive smaller units in worse physical condition with poorer services and neighborhood amenities.[39]

4.   Poor citizens have fewer opportunities to improve their own housing than wealthier citizens because most lenders will not provide mortgages for either purchase or improvement in very low-income areas, even if the borrower has good credit standing. As a result, many poor persons either fail to improve their housing, or they are compelled to resort to much more expensive forms of financing (such as contract purchase).

5.   In most parts of the world, poor migrants to urban areas are allowed to build their own housing on vacant land at the edges of the urbanized area. As their incomes rise, they

often upgrade these initially substandard units into reasonably decent shelters, and the government eventually adds standard urban utilities and services. In the United States, middle-class construction standards enforced by building codes and zoning laws make new construction of low-cost housing on vacant land impossible. Instead, low-priced units must be manufactured out of existing housing through overcrowding or deterioration. Consequently, in U.S. metropolitan areas, most poor in-migrants are concentrated in older central-city neighborhoods in units which are extremely difficult to upgrade through self-help.

6.   Poor people are a minority group in the United States, so few policies or programs benefiting them are politically viable unless they provide simultaneously equal or even larger benefits for middle-income and upper-income groups. As a result, most subsidies benefit the wealthy far more than the poor. Three examples are:

HOUSING SUBSIDIES. The largest of such subsidies consists of income-tax deductions allowed for property tax and interest payments made by home owners, and the failure to tax the benefits of occupancy which are an implicit return on investment for homeowners. As a result, the per capita housing subsidy received by the wealthiest 20 per cent of the population is twice that received by the poorest 20 per cent.[40]

URBAN RENEWAL BENEFITS. Land write-downs inherent in urban renewal programs benefit mainly real estate developers, high-income renters of renewal-project housing, downtown property owners, and local governments. In contrast, such projects displace low-income families without paying adequate compensation and cause an increased shortage of housing available to these families. This compels many poor families (displaced families as well as those living nearby) to pay higher rents.

FEDERAL SEWER AND WATER GRANTS. Most of these subsidies are used in communities which have a low proportion of poor households.

7.   Schools of the lowest quality, with the least qualified teachers and often the oldest buildings and equipment, are usually concentrated in poor neighborhoods, especially in the big cities. Furthermore, wealthy suburbs spend far more per student on all aspects of education. The resulting inequality of educational opportunity tends to aggravate income inequalities.

8.   Urban highways are often deliberately routed directly through low-income areas, especially Negro neighborhoods, but bypass wealthier residential districts. The resulting displacement imposes heavy costs upon those forced to move and those living in nearby poor neighborhoods. Yet, until 1968, compensation and relocation regulations did not provide just and adequate payment for these costs. Thus, the poor paid a sizable share of the true cost of creating highways that benefit mainly wealthier suburbanites and downtown property owners.

9.   The welfare system discourages self-improvement by its nearly 100 per cent de facto tax on earned income; provides benefit levels too low for parents to create higher aspirations in their children; furthers feelings of helplessness and dependency because of its complex rules and its administration by middle-class bureaucrats; pressures husbands to separate from their families so they can get more income; and degrades many of those it serves by its surveillance procedures.

10.   Poor neighborhoods in large cities normally receive the lowest quality of city services (such as garbage collection and police protection) as measured in quality of output. Even if poor neighborhoods receive greater per capita inputs (as they do in the case of the police), the behavior (also an input) of some residents results in services for all the residents that are inferior to those obtained in wealthier neighborhoods.

11.   New jobs are being created mainly in suburban areas distant from central-city low-income areas, especially in Negro

areas. The many unemployed persons living in the central cities are therefore handicapped in getting jobs, especially since public transportation to these new job areas is rarely available. Ironically, the movement of new jobs to such outlying areas is strongly encouraged by the construction of the same urban highways that impose such unfair costs upon low-income neighborhoods, as noted above.

12.   Police practices in low-income areas maximize the probability that young men, particularly Negroes, will develop official police records for acts that would not create such records in higher-income suburbs. Yet these records may seriously impede the employment or educational opportunities of the young people concerned, thereby impairing their ultimate income-earning capabilities.

13.   Once a poor person is arrested on suspicion of any crime, existing bail practices may compel him to remain in jail for months even if he is completely innocent, simply because he cannot raise bail. This can have a devastating effect on his family's income, his ability to locate evidence in his own behalf, and his personal welfare. Middle-income and upper-income suspects almost never have to face such difficulties because they can easily raise bail.

14.   Employers frequently add unnecessary requirements to job specifications which make it harder for poor persons with little educational attainment or a past police record to qualify. Racial prejudice is another factor in the rejection of potential employees who are poor.

15.   The U.S. Employment Service and many welfare agencies designed to serve those in need tend to "cream" their potential clientele. They focus the greatest attention on those persons most likely to develop their own capabilities successfully, thus making a good record for the agencies. As a result, the poorest potential beneficiaries—those who need the most help—usually receive the least. This problem has now been

recognized and limited steps are being taken to correct it.

These institutional perversities, and many more, tend to make escape from poverty extremely difficult for many of the persons who become trapped in it by birth or changing circumstances.

6. Future Population Changes and the Urban Poor

Policies adopted now will be operative only in the future, so it is important to know how future developments are likely to alter the sizes of the various groups of urban poor analyzed in this paper. It is much easier to forecast accurately the total number of people in each relevant group (for example, central-city nonwhites over sixty-five) than the number in that group who will be poor. This is true because the future *incidence* of poverty in each group will depend upon both general economic conditions and the nature and effectiveness of specific antipoverty policies yet to be adopted.

The only available population forecasts for metropolitan areas broken down by race, age, and portion of the metropolitan area are for the period 1960–1985 as a whole. They were prepared in June 1968 by Patricia Leavey Hodge and Philip M. Hauser for the National Commission on Urban Problems.[41] These forecasts have been used for most of the data in this section.

In the author's opinion, these projections are too high because they assume a greater future increase in the total U.S. population than will actually occur. They are based upon the Census Bureau's Series C projection. That projection assumes that fertility rates similar to those in the mid-1960's will persist through 1985. But fertility rates have already declined significantly below these levels and may fall still further. Hence, all the data set forth in this chapter reflect an upward bias of an undetermined degree. Nevertheless, they are the only data available for looking at future urban poverty trends in detail. Be-

50

cause the projections used here are based on this data, readers should be aware of the likely error inherent in them. The age breakdowns used by Hodge and Hauser are not identical with those in earlier sections of this paper. Moreover, there are no readily available data useful in forecasting the number of households headed by disabled males under sixty-five, females under sixty-five, unemployed males under sixty-five, or employed males under sixty-five with very low incomes. Therefore, only general comments can be made about future trends for these groups. Finally, it should be pointed out that data concerning the spatial distribution of specific population groups within metropolitan areas (in central cities versus suburbs) are subject to significant potential error, depending on future location patterns.

Over-all Population Trends

Future population trends relevant to each group can best be evaluated in the perspective of the following over-all trends set forth by Hodge and Hauser:

—From 1960 to 1985, total U.S. population will rise 72.9 million, or 40.6 per cent. Most of this growth (65.3 million, or 89.6 per cent) will occur inside all metropolitan areas as defined in 1967.

—Within these metropolitan areas, central cities will gain only 7.4 million persons, or 12.7 per cent, but the "suburban rings" will gain 57.9 million persons, or 105.9 per cent. Thus, most metropolitan-area growth will be in the suburbs, and that growth will form 79.4 per cent of *all* U.S. population gains from 1960 to 1985.

—The nonwhite population of the United States will grow almost twice as fast as the white population (68.2 per cent versus 37.1 per cent). It will rise by 14.0 million to a total of 34.5 million in 1985. (This is a low estimate because it is based upon census data that contain an admitted undercount of at least 10 per cent). Hence, nonwhites will comprise about one out of every seven Americans in 1985.

—Most nonwhite growth (70.0 per cent) will occur within the central cities in metropolitan areas. Nonwhite population in all those cities combined will rise 9.8 million, or 94.5 per cent. This is an average of 392,000 persons per year, resulting from both natural increase and net in-migration (mostly the former). In contrast, the white population of those cities will decline 2.4 million, or at an average rate of 96,000 per year. Consequently, by 1985 all central cities combined will be 30.7 per cent nonwhite (as compared to 23 per cent in 1968). Assuming present trends continue, most of the ten largest U.S. cities and many others will have nonwhite population majorities by 1985—including Chicago, Philadelphia, Detroit, Cleveland, St. Louis, Baltimore, Newark, Oakland, and New Orleans.

—Suburban nonwhite growth from 1960 to 1985 will be larger than central-city nonwhite growth in percentage terms (140.7 per cent versus 94.5 per cent), but less than half as large absolutely (4.0 million versus 9.8 million). Nonwhite population gains will constitute 132.8 per cent of all central-city growth (since white population will fall), but only 6.9 per cent of all suburban ring growth.

—By 1985, the balance of power between suburbs and central cities will have changed dramatically. In 1960, central cities were larger than suburban rings (58.2 million versus 54.7 million), and therefore contained a higher proportion of the total U.S. population (32.5 per cent versus 30.5 per cent). But by 1985, central cities will be only 58 per cent as large as suburban rings (65.6 million versus 112.6 million), and will contain a much smaller proportion of the total U.S. population (26.0 per cent versus 44.6 per cent). At that time, the suburban ring will be 93.9 per cent white, whereas central cities will be 69.3 per cent white.

—Although U.S. population will rise 40.6 per cent from 1960 to 1985, not all age groups will expand to the same degree. The fastest growth will occur among those fifteen to forty-four (57.2 per cent) and those sixty-five and over (50.8 per cent). Slower-than-average growth will occur among those under fifteen (30.5 per cent) and those forty-five to sixty-four (19.0 per cent). Thus there will be an enormous surge of relatively young people entering the working force, but a shortage of experienced workers and executives. And the elderly group will expand much faster proportionally than the school-age population. Similar relationships will exist within the metropolitan-area population, as shown in Table 18.

—Although steady migration of nonwhites out of the South will occur from 1960 to 1985, the base for continued migration after 1985 will be almost as large as it was in 1960. Southern nonmetropolitan, nonwhite population was 6.2 million in 1960, and will be 6.1 million in 1985. A decline in fertility rates among nonwhites will cause out-migration after 1985 to slow down, but it will not necessarily disappear.

Table 18. **Population Growth by Age Group Within All Metropolitan Areas: 1960–1985**

Age Group	Total	White	Nonwhite
All Ages	57.8%	51.6%	104.5%
Under 15	49.1	40.9	100.7
15–44	74.0	67.2	123.9
45–64	31.4	28.2	60.4
65 and over	75.5	72.1	118.8

Specific Population Trends

The following facts and observations are relevant to the likely future size of the specific groups dealt with in this paper:

THE URBAN ELDERLY. The number of elderly persons in metropolitan areas will rise sharply (75.5 per cent) by 1985. But 89.6 per cent of this increase will occur in the suburbs. Both white and nonwhite elderly in suburban areas will gain by over 150 per cent from 1960 to 1985, increasing in total by 6.5 million persons, or 261,000 per year.

In central cities, the white elderly population will rise only 3.0 per cent in this period (155,000, or 6,200 per year).

However, the nonwhite elderly population in those cities will more than double, rising by a total of 600,000 (108.7 per cent, or 24,000 per year). Taken together, both central city groups of elderly will expand by 755,000 (13.3 per cent), or 30,200 per year.

Although most future growth of the elderly population will occur in the suburbs, there will still be a sizable group of elderly persons in central cities by 1985—about 6.4 million as compared to 10.5 million in the suburban rings. The preponderant majority of elderly in both areas will be whites (82.1 per cent in central cities and 96.3 per cent in suburbs).

These data point to the following conclusions about the elderly urban *poor*:

Future growth of this group will consist mainly of suburban whites. That growth could be quite significant, since nearly one out of five elderly white persons in suburbs lived in poverty in 1968.

Elderly poor in central cities will probably rise only slightly, but will still comprise a significant proportion of all elderly poor (probably at least one-third in 1985).

Elderly nonwhite poor may double in number in central cities. If so, they would comprise a much more significant share of all elderly poor in those cities (perhaps one-fourth instead of one-sixth as in 1968).

URBAN CHILDREN. Although previous estimates in this paper concerning children dealt with all those under eighteen, the data available for forecasts cover only those under fifteen. It will therefore be assumed that percentage changes in the under-fifteen group are roughly similar to those which would apply to the under-eighteen group if they were available.

The number of children under fifteen will grow by 49.1 per cent in all U.S. metropolitan areas from 1960 to 1985. About 86 per cent of this growth (14.6 million children) will occur in the suburban rings. It will consist mainly (over 90 per cent) of white children. In 1968, about 94 per cent of all white suburban children under eighteen did *not* live in poverty. Nevertheless, there would be more than one million additional poor white children in suburbs if this same percentage remained applicable through 1985.

In central cities, the number of white children under fifteen will drop 1.1 million (8.5 per cent) by 1985, but the number of nonwhite children will rise 3.4 million (91.8 per cent). Since about one-third of nonwhite children in central cities lived in poverty in 1968, this rapid expansion will pose a very serious problem in any anti-poverty program. It might add as many as 1.4 million poor nonwhite children to central cities by 1985. The addition of children from fifteen to eighteen might raise this total as high as 1.7 million. These children will generate difficult problems involving education, crime prevention, health standards, housing, building maintenance, and other activities of vital interest to local governments.

URBAN HOUSEHOLDS HEADED BY FEMALES UNDER SIXTY-FIVE. No separate population forecasts for these households are available, so far as could be determined. However, certain deductions can be made from other available information. First, the proportion of families headed by women is much higher among nonwhites (27 per cent in 1968) than among whites (9 per cent).[42] Second, the proportion of these households living in poverty is also much higher among nonwhites (50 per cent in 1968) than among whites (22.1 per cent). Third, according to data set forth above, the nonwhite population of all central cities taken together will rise 94.5 per cent from 1960 to 1985. In the child-bearing years (fifteen to forty-four), this population will increase 112.4 per cent. Fourth, the rate of illegitimate births among nonwhites has been rising markedly in recent years, reaching 21.6 per cent in 1960 and 26.3 per cent in 1966.[43] All this indicates that there will probably be a sharp increase in poor nonwhite households headed by women in U.S. central cities—especially the largest ones—in the next two decades. To policy makers interested in eliminating poverty, particularly poverty in generations to come, these households pose the most intractable of all problems.

URBAN HOUSEHOLDS HEADED BY MALES UNDER SIXTY-FIVE. Similarly, no separate population forecasts are available for the remaining three groups of households in this study. However, the following observations are relevant to future changes in their number.

The number of poor urban *households headed by unemployed males* under sixty-five will probably increase significantly from 1960 to 1985. The metropolitan-area labor force will rise slightly faster than the metropolitan population as a whole because of the growth of the age group from fifteen to sixty-four (59.7 per cent versus 57.8 per cent for all metropolitan population). The rate of unemployment is unlikely to fall much below its present level, even if the country experiences a high degree of prosperity. Hence the number of unemployed will rise at least in proportion to the labor force even if prosperity continues. Moreover, the age group from fifteen to forty-four will rise even faster (74.0 per cent), causing young people to flood into the labor market. Unemployment, therefore, might rise significantly faster than the metropolitan labor force. This is particularly likely if the federal government pursues a price-stabilization policy that entails higher unemployment, rather than pursuing full employment with mild inflation.

Increases in the number of these households will be felt more acutely in central cities than in suburbs, because the nonwhite population in those cities will expand rapidly, especially in the age group from fifteen to forty-four (where it will rise 112.4 per cent from 1960 to 1985). And the unemployment rate among nonwhites is at least double that among whites in every age group. Significant increases in nonwhite unemployment in central cities could become linked to continued disorders, creating an extremely critical situation.

Changes in the number of poor urban households in the other two groups—*those headed by disabled males under sixty-*

five, and employed males under sixty-five with very low incomes— will also be strongly affected by the trends described above. This is true because both disability rates and the proportion of employed males under sixty-five living in poverty are much higher among nonwhites than among whites.

The fraction of households headed by disabled males under sixty-five living in poverty will be significantly influenced by future policies concerning the amount of assistance given such households. However, these households form only a small proportion of all urban poor (about 4.5 per cent in 1968, including children).

Persons living in households headed by males under sixty-five who are employed but earn low incomes will be greatly influenced by future public policies concerning minimum wages, income maintenance, and the balance between full employment and price stability. In any event, central cities will be more significantly affected by the expanding number of such households in the future than suburbs.

7. Policy Issues

The purpose of this paper is not to recommend policy but to present those factual findings upon which sound policy recommendations can be based. The findings in the preceding chapters raise a number of policy issues which should be fully deliberated before final judgments can be made and before specific policies can be formulated. These are the major issues:

Since over 40 per cent of all poor persons in metropolitan areas cannot be expected to become economically self-sustaining, significantly improved and enlarged programs of public assistance, combined with expanded child care facilities for women with dependent children, are probably the only way to remove them from poverty.

These programs could stress direct income supplementation under administrative rules which would be far simpler and less dependency-reinforcing than present welfare programs.

Such income assistance could take the form of family allowances, a negative income tax, a guaranteed minimum income, or some combination or variations of these schemes.

Provision of about 250,000 additional new jobs for unemployed adults in metropolitan areas, and sufficient hours of work for those who are under-employed, numbering about 650,000 adults, might eliminate poverty among such adults in those areas.

If these jobs paid reasonably well (about $1.70 per hour or more for the head of a four-person household) and were both full-time and year-round, filling them with these poor adults could lift about 13 per cent of all the metropolitan-area poor (1.7 million persons) out of poverty.

Because of the low skills and poor work habits of some of these adults, many of these added jobs might have to be linked to on-the-job or other training programs.

Upgrading the earnings made by presently-employed adults who are still below the poverty level could eliminate nearly one-third of all metropolitan-area poverty—or more than twice as much as results from unemployment or underemployment.
Such upgrading could require steadier work, higher minimum wages, faster advancement, better on-the-job training, and a variety of other practices.
Some of these practices could be carried out by private employers now, but most would be adopted more quickly and in greater quantity if there were government incentives.

Since over 40 per cent of all poor persons in metropolitan areas are children under eighteen, breaking the "vicious circle" of potentially self-perpetuating poverty will require greatly improved educational efforts, especially in central-city low-income areas. Developing new approaches to educating poor children might be just as important as added funding in achieving such improvement.

Basic institutional changes in low-income areas will be required if there is to be an effective attack upon urban poverty. These might include new credit-buying laws, easier availability of mortgage financing, improvements in the quality of city services, altered requirements for low-skilled jobs, less stringent bail practices, better transportation linking low-income, central-city areas and suburban job centers, more just compensation and relocation practices by federally-supported agencies, less "creaming" by agencies designed to serve the poor, and revised welfare practices.

Costly programs will be needed if there is to be any effective attack upon urban poverty. The cost of eliminating poverty or even reducing it significantly would have to be borne by society as a whole. The amount involved would depend upon exactly what remedies are adopted and to what degree, but it could exceed $5.0 billion per year (not counting any extensions to poor persons outside metropolitan areas).[44]

Poverty in metropolitan areas imposes a disproportionate financial burden upon central-city governments. This might be offset by some form of outside financial aid not dependent upon local property taxation.

Notes

1. This conclusion assumes that one-fourth of all households headed by females under sixty-five and containing children can be expected to earn sufficient incomes to become self-sustaining above the poverty level. If no such households can be expected to do this, then the total would be 54.4 per cent, instead of 46.5 per cent.

2. These groups are not entirely mutually exclusive, since children under eighteen are found as members of all the other groups. However, we have separated the children under eighteen from the other members of the four other types of households in some of our calculations, and put them back into those households in others. This will be clear from the context in each case.

3. This definition was originally worked out and explained by Mollie Orshansky in "Counting the Poor: Another Look at the Poverty Profile," *Social Security Bulletin* (January 1965), pp. 3-29; and in "Who's Who Among the Poor: A Demographic View of Poverty," *Social Security Bulletin* (June 1965), pp. 3-32. A revised definition, incorporating changes in the method of adjusting the poverty thresholds for annual cost of living fluctuations and in the poverty income differentials between farm and nonfarm families, was adopted in 1969. A description of the revised definition of poverty appears in U.S. Bureau of the Census, *Revision in Poverty Statistics, 1959 to 1968*, Current Population Reports, Series P-23, No. 28 (Washington, D.C.: U.S. Government Printing Office, August 12, 1969).

4. U.S. Bureau of the Census, *Poverty in the United States: 1959 to 1968*, Current Population Reports, Series P-60, No. 68 (Washington, D.C.: U.S. Government Printing Office, January 1970), p. 11.

5. United Nations. Statistical Office, *Yearbook of National Accounts Statistics, 1968* (New York, 1969).

6. U.S. Bureau of Labor Statistics, *Three Standards of Living for an Urban Family of Four Persons, Spring 1967*, Bulletin No. 1570-5 (Washington, D.C.: U.S. Government Printing Office, 1969); and Jean C. Brackett, "New BLS Budgets Provide Yardsticks for Measuring Family Living Costs," *Monthly Labor Review* (April 1969), pp. 3-16.

7. Real Estate Research Corporation, unpublished report to the U.S. Department of Housing and Urban Development (Chicago: 1968).

8. This subject is discussed at length by Herman Miller, "Changes in the Number and Composition of the Poor," in Conference on Poverty in America, *Poverty in America*, edited by Margaret S. Gordon (San Francisco: Chandler Pub. Co., 1965), pp. 81-101.

9. Robert Hunter, *Poverty* (New York: Macmillan Co., 1904), p. 52.

10. Robert J. Lampman, "Income Distribution and Poverty," in Conference on Poverty in America, *op. cit.*, pp. 102-111; and U.S. Bureau of the Census, *Income in 1968 of Families and Persons in the United States*, Current Population Reports, Series P-60, No. 66 (Washington, D.C.: U.S. Government Printing Office, December 23, 1969), p. 22.

11. Mollie Orshansky, "Counting the Poor, Before and After Federal Income-Support Programs," in U.S. Congress. Joint Economic Committee, *Old Age*

Income Assurance. Part II, Aged Population and Retirement Income Programs (Washington, D.C.: U.S. Government Printing Office, December 1967), pp. 177-231. An earlier study based on data for 1961 was by Christopher ·Green, *Negative Taxes and the Poverty Problem* (Washington, D.C.: Brookings Institution, 1967).

12. U.S. Bureau of the Census, *Poverty in the United States: 1959 to 1968, op. cit.*, Table H.

13. The main sources of the data in this and the following ·chapters are the tabulations prepared by the Bureau of the Census from a current population survey conducted in March 1969; these tabulations enumerate the poverty in metropolitan areas. In addition, two reports of the Bureau cited in Notes 4 and 10 are also used extensively. Hereafter, the sources of the data are the same as these tabulations and reports unless cited.

14. The metropolitan population in this study is based on Standard Metropolitan Statistical Areas as defined in the 1960 Census and does not include any subsequent additions or changes.

15. U.S. Bureau of the Census, *Revision in Poverty Statistics, 1959 to 1968, op. cit.*

16. U.S. Bureau of the Census, *Income in 1968 of Families and Persons in the United States, op. cit.*

17. Lenore Epstein Bixby, Janet H. Murray, and Erdman Palmore, "The Aged Population: Economic Status," in U.S. Congress. Joint Economic Committee, *op. cit.*, pp. 1-52.

18. *Social Security Bulletin* (December 1969), Table Q-4.

19. *Social Security Bulletin* (December 1969), Table M-12.

20. Mollie Orshansky, "Counting the Poor, Before and After Federal Income-Support Programs," in U.S. Congress. Joint Economic Committee, *Old Age Income Assurance, Compendium of Papers on Problems and Policy Issues in Public and Private Pension Systems, part II, Aged Population and Retirement Income Programs*, pp. 177-231.

21. For the three groups of male-headed households listed in this table, the number of children in each group is estimated by distributing the total number of children in male-headed families by the number of families in each group.

22. U.S. Department of Agriculture, *Dietary Levels of Households in the United States, Spring 1965* (Washington, D.C.: U.S. Government Printing Office, July 1969).

23. Citizens' Board of Inquiry into Hunger and Malnutrition in the United States, *Hunger, U.S.A.* (Washington, D.C.: New Community Press, 1968); Alan D. Berg, "Malnutrition and National Development," *Foreign Affairs* (October 1967), pp. 126-136; Peter Gwynne, "Mental Effects of Malnutrition," *Technology Review* (May 1967), pp. 23-27; and Joshua Lederberg, "Evidence Links Poor Diet to Forever-Stunted Minds," *Washington Post* (January 27, 1968), p. A13.

24. U.S. Commission on Civil Rights, *Racial Isolation in the Public Schools* (Washington, D.C.: U.S. Government Printing Office, 1967); and U.S. Office of Education, *Equality of Educational Opportunity* (Washington, D.C.: U.S. Government Printing Office, 1966).

25. Selma Fraiberg, "The Origins of Human Bonds," *Commentary* (December 1967), pp. 47-57.
26. Martin Warren and Sheldon Berkowitz, "The Employability of AFDC Mothers and Fathers," *Welfare in Review* (July-August 1969), pp. 1-7.
27. U.S. Bureau of the Census, *Poverty in the United States: 1959 to 1968, op. cit.*, Table 5.
28. U.S. President's Commission on Income Maintenance Programs, *Poverty Amid Plenty: The American Paradox* (Washington, D.C.: U.S. Government Printing Office, November 1969), p. 30.
29. U.S. Department of Health, Education and Welfare. Office of the Assistant Secretary for Planning and Evaluation, *Income and Benefit Programs* (Washington, D.C.: U.S. Government Printing Office, October 1966).
30. U.S. National Advisory Commission on Civil Disorders, *Report* (Washington, D.C.: U.S. Government Printing Office, March 1, 1968).
31. Among the supporters of this viewpoint are Daniel Patrick Moynihan and Edward Banfield.
32. Elliot Liebow, *Tally's Corner: A Study of Negro Streetcorner Men* (Boston: Little, Brown and Co., 1967).
33. U.S. Advisory Council on Public Welfare, *Having the Power, We Have the Duty: Report to the Secretary of Health, Education, and Welfare* (Washington, D.C.: U.S. Government Printing Office, June 29, 1966).
34. The Social Security Act of 1935 was amended in 1967 (Public Law 90-248, signed by President Johnson on January 2, 1968). Under the public assistance program known as Aid to Families with Dependent Children (AFDC), this revision provided that, effective July 1, 1969, "the State agency shall with respect to any month disregard . . . the first $30 of the total of such earned income for such month plus one-third of the remainder of such income for such month."
35. Elliot Liebow, *op. cit.*
36. U.S. President's Commission on Income Maintenance Programs, *op. cit.*, p. 4. Ben W. Heineman was chairman of the commission.
37. U.S. Bureau of Labor Statistics, "A Study of Prices Charged in Food Stores Located in Low and Higher Income Areas of Six Large Cities, February 1966," prepared for the U.S. National Commission on Food Marketing (Washington, D.C.: 1966).
38. U.S. Federal Trade Commission, mimeographed statement of testimony by the Commissioner (Washington, D.C.: January 1968).
39. U.S. National Advisory Commission on Civil Disorders, *op. cit.*
40. Alvin L. Schorr, "National Community and Housing Policy," *The Social Service Review* (December 1965), pp. 433-443.
41. Patricia Leavey Hodge and Philip M. Hauser, *The Challenge of America's Metropolitan Population Outlook, 1960 to 1985*, U.S. National Commission on Urban Problems Research Report No. 3 (Washington, D.C.: U.S. Government Printing Office, 1968).
42. U.S. Bureau of the Census, *Income in 1968 of Families and Persons in the United States, op. cit.*, Table 12.
43. U.S. National Advisory Commission on Civil Disorders, *Report*, p. 130.

44. The total "poverty gap" for the United States in 1968 was approximately $9.85 billion. That is, this amount of income supplementation would have been necessary to lift every one of the 5.0 million poor families and 4.7 million poor unrelated individuals above the poverty threshold appropriate to each. About 51 per cent of all poor persons lived in metropolitan areas, so the metropolitan area "poverty gap" for 1968 was approximately $5.0 billion. This figure may be too high because it does not take into account possible increased earnings through greater employment. But it may also be too low because it does not include payment of training expenses associated with such employment. We assume these two errors cancel out. The true cost of eliminating urban poverty may be higher, however, because of the institutional changes required to keep poverty from reappearing and perpetuating itself as in the past.

OTHER SUPPLEMENTARY PAPERS PUBLISHED BY CED

To order CED publications please indicate number in column entitled "Copies Desired." Then mail this order form and check for total amount in envelope to Distribution Division, CED, 477 Madison Ave., New York, 10022.

Order Number   **Copies Desired**

30S .. THE ECONOMIC FUTURE OF CITY AND SUBURB
David L. Birch
June, 1970, 56 pages, 17 figures ($1.00)   _____

29S .. TOWARD A NEW HOUSING POLICY: The Legacy of the Sixties
Morton J. Schussheim
May, 1969, 76 pages, 4 figures, 2 tables. ($1.50)   _____

28S .. THE SCHOOLS AND THE CHALLENGE OF INNOVATION
William H. Allen, Charles S. Benson, Roald F. Campbell, Robert Glaser, John I. Goodlad, Philip W. Jackson, H. Thomas James, Wilbur Schramm, Lawrence M. Stolurow, J. Alan Thomas, Ralph W. Tyler, Clyde N. Carter and Maurice J. Walker; with an Introduction by Sterling M. McMurrin
January, 1969, 372 pages, 12 tables. ($4.00)*   _____

27S .. TOP MANAGEMENT DEVELOPMENT AND SUCCESSION
An exploratory study by Albert S. Glickman, Clifford P. Hahn, Edwin A. Fleishman, Brent Baxter of American Institutes for Research
November, 1968, 108 pages. ($2.00)*   _____

26S .. WHO ARE THE URBAN POOR?
Anthony Downs
September, 1970 (Revised Edition), 80 pages, 18 tables. ($1.50) _____

25S .. ECONOMIC DEVELOPMENT ISSUES: GREECE,
ISRAEL, TAIWAN, THAILAND
Diomedes D. Psilos (Greece); Nadav Halevi (Israel); Shigeto Kawano (Taiwan); Katsumi Mitani (Thailand)
July, 1968, 232 pages, 49 tables. ($4.00)*   _____

24S .. REMAKING THE INTERNATIONAL MONETARY SYSTEM: THE
RIO AGREEMENT AND BEYOND
Fritz Machlup
June, 1968, 176 pages, 2 tables. ($3.00)*   _____

23S .. FISCAL ISSUES IN THE FUTURE OF FEDERALISM
Metropolitan Case Studies; The Potential Impact of General Aid in Four Selected States; The Outlook for State and Local Finance
May, 1968, 288 pages, 56 tables. ($3.00)   _____

22S .. REGIONAL INTEGRATION AND
THE TRADE OF LATIN AMERICA
Roy Blough and Jack N. Behrman; Rómulo A. Ferrero
January, 1968, 184 pages, 14 tables. ($2.50)   _____

21S .. ECONOMIC DEVELOPMENT ISSUES:
LATIN AMERICA
Roberto Alemann (Argentina); Mario Henrique Simonsen (Brazil); Sergio Undurraga Saavedra (Chile); Hernan Echavarria (Colombia); Gustavo Romero Kolbeck (Mexico); Romulo A. Ferrero (Peru)
August, 1967, 356 pages, 74 tables. ($4.25)*   _____

SEE OTHER SIDE⟶

20S .. MEN NEAR THE TOP:
FILLING KEY POSTS IN THE FEDERAL SERVICE
John J. Corson and R. Shale Paul
April, 1966, 192 pages. ($3.00)* ———————

19S .. CRISIS IN WORLD COMMUNISM—
MARXISM IN SEARCH OF EFFICIENCY
Frank O'Brien
January, 1965, 192 pages. ($2.75)* ———————

18S .. COMMUNITY ECONOMIC DEVELOPMENT EFFORTS:
FIVE CASE STUDIES
W. Paul Brann, V. C. Crisafulli, Donald R. Gilmore,
Jacob J. Kaufman, Halsey R. Jones, Jr., J. W. Milliman,
John H. Nixon, W. G. Pinnell
December, 1964, 352 pages, 47 tables, 14 charts. ($2.75)* ———————

17S .. HOW A REGION GROWS—
AREA DEVELOPMENT IN THE U.S. ECONOMY
Harvey S. Perloff, with Vera W. Dodds
March, 1963, 152 pages, 21 charts, 23 tables. ($2.25)* ———————

16S .. THE COMMUNITY ECONOMIC BASE STUDY
Charles M. Tiebout
December, 1962, 98 pages, 6 charts, 12 tables. ($1.50) ———————

15S .. FARMING, FARMERS, AND MARKETS
FOR FARM GOODS
Karl A. Fox, Vernon W. Ruttan, Lawrence W. Witt
November, 1962, 190 pages, 16 charts, 46 tables. ($3.00) ———————

13S .. THE SOURCES OF ECONOMIC GROWTH
IN THE UNITED STATES AND THE ALTERNATIVES BEFORE US
Edward F. Denison
January, 1962, 308 pages, 4 charts, 33 tables. ($4.00) ———————

11S .. THE EDUCATION OF BUSINESSMEN
Leonard S. Silk
December, 1960, 48 pages, 9 tables. (75¢) ———————

10S .. DEVELOPING THE "LITTLE" ECONOMIES
Donald R. Gilmore
April, 1960, 160 pages, 20 tables. ($2.00) ———————

7S .. METROPOLIS AGAINST ITSELF
Robert C. Wood
March, 1959, 56 pages. ($1.00) ———————

1S .. THE ECONOMICS OF A FREE SOCIETY
William Benton
October, 1944, 20 pages. (20¢) ———————

☐ Please bill me. (Remittance requested for orders under $10.00)
☐ Please send me CED's current publications list.
☐ I should like to know how I might receive all of CED's future publications
by becoming a Participant in the CED Reader-Forum.

* Hard cover edition available. Prices on request.

About CED...

The Committee for Economic Development (CED) is an independent research and educational organization of 200 leading businessmen and educators. With the help of advisory boards of distinguished economists and social scientists, CED trustees conduct research and formulate policy recommendations in four major areas of public policy: (1) the national economy, (2) the international economy, (3) education and urban development, and (4) the management of federal, state, and local government.

CED is nonprofit, nonpartisan, and nonpolitical. It is supported largely by contributions from business, foundations, and individuals. CED's objective is to promote stable growth with rising living standards and increasing opportunities for all Americans.

The Committee for Economic Development draws its 200 trustees largely from the ranks of board chairmen and presidents of business corporations and financial institutions, and from the ranks of university presidents. These trustees are chosen for their individual capacities, for their understanding of public problems, and for their willingness to view these problems from the standpoint of the general welfare and not from that of any special interest group.

All CED policy recommendations must be approved by a fifty-man group of trustees, the Research and Policy Committee, which alone can speak for the organization. These recommendations are set forth in Statements on National Policy and are the result of months of research, discussion, and policy formulation. In connection with the publication of a statement, CED often publishes documents originally prepared by scholars as background papers but deemed worthy of wider circulation, as in the case of the present Supplementary Paper. Though publication of such papers must be authorized by an editorial board of trustees and academic advisors as a contribution to knowledge, the opinions and conclusions expressed are solely those of the individual authors and do not reflect the policies or views of the trustees.